Journey Through the Bible: Women of the Word

Joseph Montgomery

ISBN: 979-8-9960443-0-6 (Ebook)
ISBN: 979-8-9960443-1-3 (Paperback)
ISBN: 979-8-9960443-2-0 (Hardcover)

Front cover image by Joseph Montgomery.
Book design by Joseph Montgomery.

Printed in the United States of America.

4 Corners Fellowship Ministries
4cfministries@gmail.com

DEDICATION

This book is dedicated to all the strong, faith-filled women who have walked this earth with unwavering conviction and grace. Women that include my Grandmother, Iris Fern Kingham , who was a constant source of strength in my life. I love you, Grandma. I miss you more than words could ever adequately express. And until that blessed day when we are reunited in heaven, I will strive every day to make you proud, to honor your memory, and to carry forward the extraordinary legacy of faith, strength, and love that you so generously passed on to all who were blessed to know you.

Dear Vigilant Reader,

In an age saturated with information and influential voices, it is of paramount importance to cultivate a spirit of thoughtful discernment. This means resisting the temptation to place blind, unquestioning faith in the words of any single person, regardless of their apparent authority, captivating charisma, or the size of their following. This critical principle applies universally—to celebrated theologians, beloved pastors, popular authors, and even to the very words you are reading now. Every human source, no matter how well-intentioned, is fallible and filtered through the lens of personal experience, tradition, and cultural context. We must recognize that we are the beneficiaries of an immense and historically rare blessing: widespread, personal access to the Holy Scriptures in our own languages. This was not always the case. For centuries during the early church and the Middle Ages, the Bible was largely confined to scholarly languages like Greek, Latin, and Hebrew, accessible only to the clergy and educated elite. Ordinary believers relied almost entirely on second-hand teaching, which was sometimes incomplete or distorted. The ability to own, read, and study the Bible for ourselves is a privilege secured through tremendous sacrifice, including the work of translators like Jerome and Wycliffe, and reformers who risked—and often lost—their lives for this cause.

Therefore, it is not only a privilege but a profound responsibility to prioritize first-hand engagement with the biblical text. Make a disciplined practice of reading and studying the Bible for yourself. Do not be content with a diet of only pre-digested sermons, commentary, or devotional excerpts. Engage directly with the source material. In doing so, establish the Scriptures as your ultimate plumb line, your final authority, and your unchanging standard against which all other truth claims must be measured. When you encounter any teaching, doctrinal statement, or piece of advice—whether from a pulpit, a book, or a blog—adopt the noble practice of the Bereans, who "examined the Scriptures every day to see if what Paul said was true" (Acts 17:11). Scrutinize everything by comparing it to the consistent and eternal truth revealed in God's Word.

Finally, acknowledge that intellectual study alone is insufficient. The Bible is a spiritual book that requires spiritual discernment. Actively and prayerfully seek the wisdom and guidance of the Holy Spirit, who was promised by Jesus to "guide you into all the truth" (John 16:13). It is the Spirit who illuminates the text, convicts the heart, and transforms knowledge into genuine understanding and godly application. By combining diligent personal study with dependent prayer for divine illumination, you build a faith that is resilient, deeply personal, and firmly anchored in the unchanging truth of God.

Pastor Joseph C. Montgomery

TABLE OF CONTENTS:

Women of the Word

In this comprehensive study, we will embark on a detailed exploration of the vast majority of women featured within the pages of the Bible. Our approach will be both chronological and canonical, beginning our journey in the foundational narratives of the Old Testament and progressing systematically through to the transformative events of the New Testament.

It is crucial, however, to first define the scope of "almost all." This qualification is made with the utmost respect for the countless female figures who, though instrumental, remain in the historical shadows. Scripture contains a significant number of unnamed women—individuals with profound impact but no recorded name or detailed history. These include pivotal figures like Noah's wife, who endured the unimaginable trial of the Flood and helped repopulate the earth, and his daughters-in-law, who carried the future of humanity in their wombs within the safety of the Ark. Their silent strength was a cornerstone of God's plan for renewal.

Furthermore, there are women who are granted a name but little else, providing only the faintest glimpse into their existence. A prime example can be found in the early genealogies of Genesis. Lamech (a descendant of Cain, distinct from the later Lamech in Seth's line) is noted to have two wives: Adah and Zillah (Genesis 4:19-22). The text tells us Adah bore Jabal, "the father of those who live in tents and raise livestock," and Zillah bore Jubal, "the father of all who play the harp and flute." While their sons' legacies in nomadic culture and music are noted, Adah and Zillah themselves vanish from the narrative. We know their names and their biological contribution, but their stories, thoughts, and faith remain a mystery.

It is to these women—the unnamed and the under-described—that this study wishes to pay solemn respect. We acknowledge that the biblical record, while divinely inspired, is a product of its ancient historical context and does not always elaborate on the lives of every individual. Yet, their presence and contributions are undeniable threads in the grand tapestry of God's word. We see you, and we honor your role.

This is especially true for the foundational matriarchs of the Messianic line. To the wife of Shem, son of Noah: though your name is lost to history, from your lineage would eventually spring forth Abraham, David, and ultimately, Jesus Christ, the Savior of the world. Your existence was a critical, God-ordained link in the chain of redemption. We may not know your name, but we see your indispensable contribution to the fulfillment of God's ultimate promise.

Therefore, as we proceed to examine the stories of the more well-known women—from Eve and Sarah to Ruth and Esther, from Mary the mother of Jesus to Mary Magdalene and Priscilla—we do so with the foundational understanding that their narratives stand upon the shoulders of many faithful women whose names heaven knows, even if earth has forgotten them.

Section One: Women of the Old Testament

While the grand narratives of kings, prophets, and warriors often dominate the landscape of Scripture, it is a profound truth that this sacred text is itself carried on the resilient shoulders of women. Their names—Sarah, Miriam, Rahab, Esther, Ruth—often echo more softly through its pages than the thunderous pronouncements of patriarchs, yet the resonance of their influence ripples powerfully across centuries, shaping the very lineage and character of faith. They are not mere footnotes or supporting actors; they are pillars often hidden in plain sight, bearing immense weight with quiet strength.

We find these women not in one type of place, but in every conceivable context of ancient life. They stand at the community well, the social and spiritual hub, drawing water and drawing out God's promises. They stand in the vast and terrifying wilderness, facing scarcity and fear with unwavering trust. They walk the polished floors of palaces, leveraging their influence in the halls of power to alter the course of history. They dwell in humble, dusty tents, shaping the future of nations from the intimate space of the home. Some, like Queen Esther, are celebrated in dramatic festivals of deliverance. Others, like the shrewd servant Abigail or the resilient widow of Zarephath, operate in near-anonymity, their crucial interventions known only to a few yet pivotal to the divine story.

Their roles are as diverse as their settings: founding matriarchs who bore the weight of a promise yet unborn; fearless prophetesses who spoke truth to power; cunning queens who risked everything for their people; humble servants whose simple obedience unlocked miracles; and profound survivors of trauma and loss who rebuilt their lives with breathtaking courage. Each one, regardless of her status or recognition, reveals a unique and essential facet of God's heart—His faithfulness, His justice, His compassion, His strategic providence—and advances His grand, unfolding plan of redemption in ways both bold and subtle.

To journey through the Old Testament, therefore, is to do more than study ancient history; it is to encounter real women who wrestled in the dust and grit of real life. They grappled with the agonizing tension between divine promise and prolonged pain. They faced moments that demanded raw courage in the face of overwhelming fear. They walked paths of faithful obedience even when every step was shrouded in profound uncertainty. Their lives are not distant relics preserved under glass; they are mirrors held up to our own souls, offering us clear, compelling glimpses of a dynamic faith lived in real time, amid real struggle, anchored in a real and steadfast hope.

Through their stories, we learn a transformative truth: that the God of the universe has a divine propensity for noticing the unnoticed. He does not overlook the overlooked. He specializes in weaving threads of glorious redemption through the lives and stories of those the world might easily dismiss—the foreigner, the barren woman, the outcast, the widow, the second-class citizen. He inverts earthly expectations, choosing the weak to lead the strong and the foolish to confound the wise.

This exploration is an invitation to step intentionally into their stories—to sit with them at the well, to stand beside them in the palace court, to share their fear in the wilderness. These are stories of resilience that defies despair, devotion that alters destinies, wisdom that outsmarts empires, and boldness that saves nations. They are not silent stories; they are narratives that still speak with clarity and power into our modern complexities. As you meet these women, may you discover not only the fascinating details of who they were, but, more importantly, what their journeys reveal about the character of the God who saw them in their obscurity, called them by name, and worked through their faithfulness in truly extraordinary ways.

The First Matriarch: Eve

Our exploration into the foundational narratives of the Bible begins, aptly, in the book of Genesis. Here, amidst the grand account of cosmic and terrestrial creation, we encounter the profound introduction of the first woman, a figure of immense significance. The story unfolds in Genesis Chapter 2, which provides a more focused, ground-level view of humanity's origin, complementing the cosmic scope of Chapter 1.

Following the creation of the lush Garden of Eden, God forms ha-'adam (האדם)—a term meaning "the man" or "humankind" from the dust of the ground. God places him in the garden to work and keep it, establishing a relationship between humanity and creation. At this point, God makes a striking divine observation: "It is not good for the man to be alone." This declaration is profoundly meaningful, as it is the first thing in the creation narrative labeled "not good." Despite the man existing in a perfect world, in unbroken fellowship with God Himself, a fundamental lack is identified. God immediately resolves this, proclaiming, "I will make him a helper comparable to him."

The term "helper" (`ezer in Hebrew - עֵזֶר) is crucial and is often misunderstood. It does not imply a subordinate assistant. In fact, the same Hebrew word is frequently used to describe God Himself as humanity's helper (e.g., Psalm 121:1-2). It signifies a strong, indispensable ally, a necessary and powerful support. "Comparable to him" (often translated as "fit for him" or "corresponding to him") translates the Hebrew kenegdo, meaning "opposite as to him" or "a counterpart to him." This denotes not sameness, but a complementary partnership—another being who stands face-to-face with him, equal in dignity and value, yet different in function and nature.

To illustrate this point, God parades the animals and birds before the man, and he exercises his God-given authority by naming them. This act of naming is an exercise in discernment and categorization. Through this process, a deep, experiential truth dawns on the man: "for Adam there was not found a helper comparable to him." Among all the living creatures, each wonderful in its own right, none possessed the capacity for the kind of relational, intellectual, and spiritual partnership he inherently needed. He recognized his own solitude in a world of non-corresponding beings.

It is at this moment of recognized need that God performs a profound and intimate act. He causes a "deep sleep" (tardemah - תַּרְדֵּמָה) to fall upon the man. This is not a normal sleep; it is a divinely induced, supernatural state, often used in Scripture for times of divine revelation or intervention. While the man is in this vulnerable, passive state, God performs the first "surgery." The text states: "He took one of his ribs, and closed up the flesh in its place."

From this rib*, God "built" (the Hebrew word banah - בָּנָה implies a careful, purposeful construction) a woman. He then personally presents her to the man. Upon awakening and seeing her, the man erupts in the first recorded words of poetry in the Bible, a cry of joyous recognition:

“This is now bone of my bones And flesh of my flesh; She shall be called Woman (Ishah), Because she was taken out of Man (Ish).”

His declaration is one of intimate connection and shared essence. She is not a foreign being; she is of his very self. He names her Ishah, the feminine form of Ish (man), establishing their fundamental equality and inextricable link.

Before we proceed further into this foundational narrative, it's crucial that we stop and critically examine a specific, deeply ingrained detail: the creation of Eve from Adam's "rib." This may be a challenging notion for many, as it is a story taught from childhood and embedded in our cultural and religious lexicon. However, I must be forthright: after considerable study, I do not believe the ancient text intended to convey that God physically removed a bony rib from Adam to fashion the first woman. This interpretation, I argue, is a product of translational limitation rather than divine intent.

Allow me to present the evidence that has led me to this conclusion. As always, my strongest encouragement to you is to not simply accept my word as truth. I urge you to engage in your own research, to interrogate my claims, and to verify them against scholarly resources and the original languages. A faith that questions and seeks understanding is a resilient faith.

The entire crux of this issue rests on the original Hebrew language used in Genesis 2:21-22. The English word "rib" is a translation of the Hebrew word "tsela" (צֵלָע). To understand what the biblical author truly meant, we must look at how this word is used throughout the Hebrew Bible. "Tsela" appears approximately 40 times in the Old Testament, and its meaning in the vast majority of these instances is not anatomical. It is most commonly translated as "side"—referring to the side of a structure like the Ark of the Covenant (Exodus 25:12), the side of a building (Ezekiel 41:5), or the side of a hill or mountain. It denotes a lateral part of something larger.

Critically, this word is used in an anatomical sense only once—in the story of Eve's creation. This outlier status should immediately prompt us to question if "rib" is the most accurate rendering. If the author's primary intent was to specify a literal, bony rib, a more precise word existed in the Semitic lexicon: the Aramaic word "ʿălaʿ" (עֲלַע). We see this word used unmistakably in Daniel 7:5, which describes a bear raised up on one side with three ribs in its mouth. Here, in a context undeniably about anatomy, the author chose "ʿălaʿ," not "tsela." This is a powerful piece of linguistic evidence suggesting that "tsela" in Genesis carries a different, broader meaning.

Therefore, we can reasonably conclude that "tsela" likely meant something closer to "side" or a "portion taken from the side." The text clearly states that God took this tsela and "closed up the flesh in its place." This act of closing the flesh is significant. The "God used half of Adam" interpretation presents a logical challenge: if God removed an entire half of Adam (as some scholars suggest based on "side"), the text gives no indication that this massive wound was healed or that Adam was made whole again; it only mentions closing the flesh. Conversely, if it was just a small rib bone, the procedure described seems unnecessarily invasive for a creator God who spoke the universe into existence. The text is curiously silent on the size of the incision, focusing instead on the action of taking and then closing.

So, if not a rib, and if not a literal half, what was this "tsela" from Adam's side? Based on the evidence within the text and our modern understanding of biology, I propose a compelling interpretation: God took a sample of living tissue from Adam's side to extract his genetic code—his DNA—to create Eve.

This view elegantly reconciles the linguistic and narrative details. The surgical procedure of opening the flesh makes perfect sense for obtaining a cellular sample. The act of "closing up the flesh" describes a minor incision that heals cleanly. Most importantly, it honors the profound theological truth embedded in the story: that Eve was made from Adam, literally of his same substance and essence. Deoxyribonucleic acid (DNA) is the fundamental blueprint of life, the biological instruction set that defines our very being. The iconic double helix structure is a helix curve—a sophisticated, divinely engineered pattern containing all the information needed to construct a human.

In this act, God did not merely clone Adam. He used the foundational blueprint—Adam's DNA—to craft a corresponding and complementary human being: Woman. This explains their fundamental sameness ("bone of my bones, flesh of my flesh") and their beautiful differentiation. It presents a creator who works with intentional, intricate science, using the very fabric of biological life as His material. This interpretation doesn't diminish the miracle; it elevates it, revealing a process of breathtaking genius and purpose that resonates with the physical world He himself designed.

*****

Now that we understand the circumstances of Eve's creation—crafted as a perfect companion from Adam's own flesh and placed as co-occupent in the lush paradise of Eden—we turn to the pivotal moment of her tragic downfall. This event, detailed in Genesis Chapter 3, transcends the simple "forbidden fruit story" many learned in Sunday school, revealing a complex narrative of temptation, free will, and profound consequences.

The scene opens not with Eve seeking rebellion, but with a cunning interrogation. The Serpent, described as "more crafty than any other beast of the field," initiates a deceptive dialogue. He does not outright deny God's command but subtly twists it into a question, asking Eve, "Did God actually say, 'You shall not eat of any tree in the garden'?" This masterful manipulation immediately shifts the focus from God's generosity (you may eat from every tree except one) to a perceived restriction, planting a seed of doubt about the Creator's goodness.

Eve, in her innocence, corrects the Serpent but adds her own interpretation to the divine command, stating that they must not even touch the fruit, lest they die. This slight embellishment reveals a subtle human tendency to build fences around God's law, a practice that can sometimes make His commands seem more harsh than they are. Seizing on this, the Serpent moves from distortion to direct contradiction. He flatly denies the consequence of death and presents a tantalizing alternative motive for God's rule: divine jealousy. "You will not surely die," he hissed. "For God knows that when you eat of it your eyes will be opened, and you will be like God, knowing good and evil."

This was the masterstroke. The temptation was not merely for a piece of fruit, but for a perceived upgrade in existence—autonomy, wisdom, and divinity itself. The fruit, once simply forbidden, now appeared "good for food," "a delight to the eyes," and, most potently, "desired to make one wise." In that moment, Eve's trust in God's word was weighed against the enticing promise of the Serpent's word, and her desire for wisdom tipped the scale. She took the fruit and ate.

The immediate aftermath was not the godlike enlightenment she might have imagined, but a shocking and shameful self-awareness. "Then the eyes of both were opened." Their pristine innocence shattered, and their first and most profound realization was of their own nakedness and vulnerability. The harmonious relationship between husband and wife was now fractured by shame, and they scrambled to sew together crude covering from fig leaves—a pathetic human attempt to solve a divinely-sized problem.

This internal rupture was followed by the ultimate relational break: when they heard the sound of God walking in the garden, they hid themselves among the trees. The Creator who had been their joy and companion was now someone to be feared and avoided. The subsequent divine inquiry—"Where are you?"—was not because God did not know, but to give them a chance to confess. Instead, it triggered history's first blame-shifting exercise: Adam blamed Eve, and by extension, God Himself ("the woman whom you gave to be with me"), and Eve, in turn, blamed the Serpent.

Thus, what began with a whispered doubt culminated in a cataclysmic unraveling of the created order. Eve's downfall was not a simple act of disobedience but a fundamental shift in the human condition—the entrance of sin, shame, fear, and death into the world, forever altering humanity's relationship with God, with each other, and with creation itself.
Following the fraught scene in the Garden of Eden, where Adam, Eve, and the serpent each deflected responsibility for their transgression, God pronounced a series of consequential judgments. These are not merely arbitrary punishments but a divine delineation of a broken world order, a description of how the perfect harmony of creation will now be fractured by sin.

The curses are delivered in the order of the offense. God first addresses the serpent, who embodied the voice of temptation. His curse is the most severe: he is condemned to an existence of humiliation and ultimate defeat, forced to crawl on its belly and eat dust. Most significantly, God declares an eternal enmity between the serpent's offspring and the woman's offspring, prophesying a future conflict where a descendant of Eve will ultimately crush the serpent's head—a pivotal moment of proto-evangelism, or the first gospel, foreshadowing the victory of Christ.

The judgment then turns to the woman. The profound joy and purpose of bringing forth new life—an act that was meant to be a pure reflection of God's creativity—will now be intertwined with intense pain and suffering. Furthermore, the harmonious partnership between man and woman is corrupted into a relationship of struggle and domination. God declares that her desire will be for her husband, yet he will rule over her, inaugurating a painful power dynamic that would characterize countless human relationships thereafter.

For Adam, the very ground from which he was taken is now cursed because of him. His God-given vocation to work and keep the Garden, which was once a source of fulfillment and joy, becomes a relentless, frustrating struggle. He will now labor against a resistant earth, battling thorns and thistles to eke out a meager sustenance until he ultimately returns to the dust from which he was formed.

It is crucial to understand these pronouncements within the full scope of biblical theology. They describe the catastrophic consequences of the Fall, but they are not the final word on humanity's destiny. Scripture provides a path of redemption. As highlighted in the New Testament, in 1 Timothy 2:15, a verse often debated by scholars, it states: “Nevertheless she will be saved in childbearing if they continue in faith, love, and holiness, with self-control.” This is not a simplistic or transactional promise that physical childbirth guarantees salvation. Rather, it is a profound metaphor for the entire life of faith. It points to the ultimate "childbearing"—the birth of the Messiah, Jesus Christ, from the line of Eve—through whom salvation comes. For both women and men, the path to being spared the eternal consequences of sin is the same: to live a life characterized by faith in God, love for others, pursuit of holiness, and self-control, ultimately made possible through grace. This call to faithful servitude is the universal antidote to the curse of separation from God.

(The specific nature of the serpent's curse, including its identity as Satan and the Messianic promise, will be explored in greater depth in a later chapter.)

Finally, Genesis chapter 3 closes with two solemn, yet significant, acts that solidify humanity's new reality. First, Adam names his wife Eve (Chavah in Hebrew), which means "life" or "living." Even in the midst of judgment and mortality, this name is a testament of hope. Second, and most devastatingly, they are exiled from the Garden of Eden. To prevent them from eating from the Tree of Life and thus living forever in their fallen state, God banishes them, stationing mighty cherubim and a flaming sword that turned every way to guard the way back. This expulsion was an act of severe mercy, sealing humanity's separation from God's direct presence and launching them into a world now shadowed by toil, pain, and death—yet never without the enduring whisper of the promised hope of redemption.

*****

We bring our exploration of the life of Eve, humanity's first matriarch, to a close with a reflection on the most profound and heartbreaking anguish a mother could ever be asked to endure: the death of a child by the hand of another. Her story, born from the dust of paradise and the pain of exile, reaches its tragic crescendo in the conflict between her own sons.

The biblical account in Genesis Chapter 4 begins with a flicker of maternal joy, noting the births of her first two children: Cain, whose name echoes the act of creation, "I have acquired a man from the LORD," and later, his brother Abel, a name meaning "breath" or "vapor," a haunting portent of his fleeting life. The boys grew, their paths diverging as they entered adulthood. Cain, the elder, followed in the vocational footsteps of his father, Adam, becoming a "tiller of the ground," a farmer who wrestled sustenance from the unforgiving soil outside Eden. Abel, in contrast, became the Bible's first recorded shepherd, a keeper of flocks, a tender of living beings.

Scripture then collapses an unknowable stretch of time—years, perhaps decades of family life, shared meals, and childhood memories—into a single, fateful moment. The brothers each bring an offering to God. Cain presents the fruit of his labor: a portion of his harvest. Abel brings the firstborn of his flock, the choicest and most valuable of his possessions, offering their fat portions as a sacrifice. In a divine response that has puzzled readers for millennia, God "respected Abel and his offering, but He did not respect Cain and his offering."

The rejection was a public, soul-crushing humiliation. Cain's face darkened, his countenance fell, and a furnace of anger and jealous bitterness ignited within him. It is here that we find a profoundly tender and often overlooked lesson. God, rather than turning away from Cain's sulking rage, approached him. He engaged the hurting young man with poignant, fatherly questions: "Why are you angry? And why has your countenance fallen?" God's response was not one of final condemnation but of gracious instruction and a clear path to redemption. He said, "If you do well, will you not be accepted? And if you do not do well, sin lies at the door. And its desire is for you, but you should rule over it."

In this crucial moment, God consoles Cain, assuring him that a single failed offering is not a life sentence. The door to acceptance remains wide open; all he must do is choose to "do well" moving forward. Simultaneously, God issues a stark warning: unchecked anger is a dangerous gateway. Sin is personified as a predatory beast, "crouching at the door," its desire to dominate and destroy him. Yet, even in this warning, there is a bedrock of reassurance—God affirms Cain's God-given agency and strength, telling him he has the power to "rule over it."

Tragically, we know the choice Cain made. Consumed by the very sin he was warned to master, he lured his brother Abel into a field and, in an act of brutal violence, became the world's first murderer. The joyous sounds of her sons' voices were now replaced for Eve by a silence broken only by the divine voice calling out to Cain, "Where is Abel your brother?" and the dreadful answer, "I do not know. Am I my brother's keeper?"

The text does not give us an explicit scene of Eve's mourning. It doesn't need to. The depth of her devastation is etched into a single, heart-wrenching verse later on: "And Adam knew his wife again, and she bore a son and named him Seth, 'For God has appointed another seed for me instead of Abel, whom Cain killed.'" The name Seth means "appointed," and in bestowing it, Eve reveals a mother's shattered heart desperately seeking solace. From her perspective, Seth was a divine replacement, a new son appointed to fill the agonizing void left by Abel's murder. Yet, from God's eternal perspective, Seth was appointed for a far greater purpose: to become the faithful line through which the promised seed—the one who would ultimately crush the serpent's head—would eventually come. In Seth, a mother's grief and God's redemptive plan converged.

The final curtain on Eve's long life is drawn without fanfare. The Bible does not record her age at death. Yet, considering the pre-flood genealogies and the remarkable age of her husband, Adam, who lived to be 930 years old, we can assume her life was one of incredible longevity. She witnessed the dawn of humanity, experienced its first joys and deepest sorrows, and lived to see her legacy—both bloody and blessed—branch out across the face of the earth. Her story is the human story: one of immense love, catastrophic loss, and the enduring, flickering hope of appointed redemption.

The Matriarch of nations: Sarah

Our biblical journey to understand the matriarch Sarah begins with a significant chronological leap. The narrative moves from the foundational stories of Adam, Eve, Cain, and Abel in Genesis Chapter 4 to the pivotal account of the Tower of Babel in Genesis Chapter 11. It is here, within the genealogy of Shem, that we first encounter her, introduced not yet as "Sarah" but as "Sarai," the wife of Abram (who has not yet been renamed Abraham). This initial introduction is strikingly brief, offering no details of her origin, lineage, or character—a silence that has fueled scholarly and rabbinic inquiry for millennia.

The biblical text itself provides only a single, tantalizing clue to her background. Later, in Genesis 20:12, Abraham, explaining his actions to Abimelech, reveals a startling piece of information: "And yet indeed she is my sister; she is the daughter of my father, but not the daughter of my mother; and she became my wife." This verse establishes Sarai as Abraham's half-sibling, both being children of Terah but from different mothers. This patriarchal family structure was not uncommon in the ancient Near East, aimed at keeping wealth and lineage within the clan. However, this solitary datum is where the Biblical account stops, leaving many questions unanswered. To delve deeper, one must turn to the vast body of Jewish exegetical tradition, particularly the Talmud.

For those unfamiliar, the Talmud is far more than a historical document; it is the central pillar of Rabbinic Judaism. Compiled and redacted between approximately the 3rd and 5th centuries CE (Common Era, a critical date correction from the original text), it represents centuries of oral debate and interpretation. It consists of two primary components: the Mishnah (the written compendium of Jewish oral law) and the Gemara (a record of rabbinic analyses, commentaries, and debates on the Mishnah). Together, they form an encyclopedic work covering law, ethics, philosophy, customs, history, and folklore, representing the collective wisdom of thousands of rabbis (known as Chazal). It is considered the primary source for Halakha (Jewish law) and is second in religious authority only to the Hebrew Bible itself. It is within this rich interpretive tradition that we find additional insights into Sarai's origins. Certain Talmudic and midrashic sources (such as Megillah 14a) imply a more specific relationship: that Sarai was the daughter of Haran, who was the father of Lot. This creates a fascinating and complex family dynamic, suggesting Sarai was Lot's sister.

This immediately presents a theological and chronological puzzle. If Sarai is Haran's daughter (and thus Abram's niece), how do we reconcile this with Abraham's own clear statement in Genesis 20:12 that she is his father's daughter (i.e., his half-sister)? Before attempting to resolve this apparent contradiction, we must first establish its feasibility by returning to the Biblical chronology in Genesis 11. Genesis 11:26 (KJV) states: "And Terah lived seventy years, and begat Abram, Nahor, and Haran." The verse lists three sons, but it does not specify whether they were triplets or born sequentially over time. The subsequent verse, Genesis

11:32, reveals: "And the days of Terah were two hundred and five years: and Terah died in Haran."

If we take the numbers literally, Terah was 70 when Abram was born and died at 205, meaning Abram was 135 when his father died (205 - 70 = 135). We know from Genesis 12:4 that Abram was 75 when he left Haran after Terah's death. This creates a chronological tension that ancient interpreters solved by suggesting Terah was 70 when his firstborn (Haran) was born, and Nahor and Abram followed later. This chronology is crucial for our question. If Haran was the eldest son, born when Terah was 70, he could have been old enough to father a daughter, Sarai, while still a young man. If Sarai was born when Haran was, for example, 30, she would then be Abram's niece, but she would also be Terah's granddaughter. This seems to directly contradict Abraham's claim that she was his father's (Terah's) daughter.

Rabbinic interpretation resolves this by harmonizing the two ideas. The proposed solution is that Haran died young (a fact mentioned in Genesis 11:28), and after his death, his daughter Sarai was adopted and raised by her grandfather, Terah. In the cultural and legal context of the time, an adopted child was often considered, for all intents and purposes, the child of the adopting parent. Therefore, Abraham could truthfully refer to Sarai as "the daughter of my father" in a legal or social sense, acknowledging her adoption by Terah, while simultaneously understanding her biological lineage as the daughter of his brother Haran. This elegant solution respects both the plain meaning of Abraham's statement and the deeper layers of tradition found in the Talmud, painting a more intricate picture of the family's tragic and complex history before their destiny unfolded.

This leaves one final question: if Sarai was indeed the daughter of Haran, why isn't she listed in his genealogy in Genesis 11? The verse (11:29) states: "And Abram and Nahor took wives: the name of Abram's wife was Sarai, and the name of Nahor's wife, Milcah, the daughter of Haran the father of Milcah and the father of Iscah." Here, Haran is explicitly named as the father of Milcah and Iscah, but not Sarai. Talmudic scholars, notably in Sanhedrin 69b, offer a compelling identification: Iscah is Sarai. The suggestion is that "Iscah" (יִסְכָּה) was her given name at birth, meaning "to gaze" or "to foresee," perhaps hinting at her prophetic qualities. After her adoption by Terah, her name was changed to Sarai (שָׂרַי), meaning "my princess," signaling her elevated status within Terah's household. This name would later be elevated again by God to Sarah (שָׂרָה), "princess," denoting her destiny as the mother of nations. Thus, the verse does indeed list her, but under her original name, Iscah, solidifying the rabbinic interpretation of her true biological origins as the daughter of Haran.

*****

The opening verses of Genesis 12 mark a tectonic shift in the biblical narrative, moving from the universal story of humanity to the specific, intimate forging of a covenant people. The divine command issued to Abram is not a gentle suggestion but a stark, totalizing ultimatum: he is to sever every earthly anchor of identity and security—his country, his kinship network, and his father's household. In an honor-shame culture where lineage and land were everything, this command demanded a terrifying leap into the unknown. In response, God counters this profound loss with an even more profound, seven-fold promise: Abram will become a great nation; he will be personally blessed; his name will be made great; he will himself be a blessing; God will bless those who bless him; God will curse those who curse him; and finally, and most astonishingly, all the families of the earth will be blessed through him.

This cosmic vow, while spoken directly into Abram's ear, sent immediate and unsettling ripples throughout his entire household, landing with a particularly heavy and personal weight upon his wife, Sarai. For embedded within the grand, soaring rhetoric of "a great nation" and "innumerable descendants" was a silent, agonizing question mark hovering over her own life and body. At sixty-five years old, Sarai was not merely advanced in age; she was decades beyond the normal childbearing years, and her lifelong barrenness was both a deep private sorrow and a source of public shame in a culture that measured a woman's worth almost exclusively by her fertility. Yet, her septuagenarian husband had just irrevocably staked their entire future, abandoning all they knew, on a divine guarantee that hinged entirely on the existence of an heir she seemed biologically incapable of providing. The unspoken tension between this glorious promise and her barren reality must have been a constant, painful presence in their tent.

Despite this profound inner conflict and the monumental uncertainty of the journey ahead, Sarai's faith was not passive; it was demonstrated through decisive action. She did not hesitate, argue, or remain behind in the comparative safety of Haran. Instead, she faithfully gathered her life and accompanied her husband, their nephew Lot, and the vast entourage of servants, herds, and possessions they had accumulated on the perilous trek south toward the unfamiliar and sparsely populated land of Canaan. Her presence on that journey was a quiet but powerful testament to her steadfast loyalty—both to Abram, her husband, and to the mysterious God he had chosen to obey. She became a co-pilgrim in the promise, even if her role within it remained agonizingly unclear.

This fledgling faith, however, was soon to be tested to its absolute breaking point. Our next stop in the narrative, Genesis 12:10-20, finds the fledgling clan not reveling in a land of milk and honey, but facing a desperate crisis of survival. A severe famine, a recurring biblical motif testing faith, grips Canaan, withering the pastures and threatening their very existence. This force of nature pushes them downward, both geographically and morally, into Egypt—a powerful, opulent, and sophisticated empire. As they approached the border, the dynamic shifted profoundly. Abram, the recipient of God's covenant, was suddenly stripped of his divinely granted confidence. Now, he was merely a vulnerable nomadic herdsman, a nobody from the hinterlands, entering a foreign superpower whose customs and power structures he did not understand. Gripped by a terror that overshadowed his faith, he turned to Sarai, who was known to be a woman of striking beauty even at her age, and unveiled a plan born of pure desperation and human calculus, not divine trust.

His request was devastating: "Say you are my sister, so that I will be treated well for your sake and my life will be spared because of you." This was more than a white lie; it was a calculated, half-true deception designed for self-preservation at her direct expense. It deliberately stripped Sarai of her legally protected status as a married woman, rendering her vulnerable and available. Abram's motive was transparent: he reasoned that if the powerful Egyptians coveted her beauty, they would have no compunction about killing her husband to remove the only obstacle to taking her. By presenting her as his unmarried sister, he could potentially barter for their safe passage or even profit from a lavish bride price, all while ensuring his own survival. In this pivotal moment, the man who had just received an unconditional covenant from the Almighty God, the maker of heaven and earth, resorted to the cheapest kind of human cunning. He effectively leveraged his wife's beauty, safety, and virtue as a bargaining chip to save his own skin, a decision of profound moral failure that would trigger a chain of events leading to their humiliating expulsion from Egypt by a righteously indignant Pharaoh.

*****

Our narrative, having swiftly passed over the events of the intervening chapters, now returns its focus to the central tent of Abram and Sarai. Despite the profound promises of God—that Abram would become a great nation and his offspring would be as countless as the stars—a heavy and seemingly unbreakable silence filled their home. The promise remained unfulfilled, and with each passing year, the weight of Sarai's barrenness grew more oppressive, a private grief that overshadowed the divine covenant.

It is against this backdrop of strained hope and cultural shame that Chapter 16 opens, introducing a pivotal and complex figure: Hagar, an Egyptian maidservant. She enters the biblical narrative not as a principal actor, but as a piece of property, a solution born of human desperation rather than divine instruction. Following the custom of the time, Sarai, feeling her age and the pressure to provide an heir, devises a plan. She approaches Abram and declares, “Behold now, the LORD has prevented me from bearing children. Go in to my servant; it may be that I shall obtain children by her.” Abram, perhaps also wrestling with doubt in the delayed promise, acquiesces to his wife’s proposal.

Hagar, a woman with no agency in the matter, is given to Abram as a secondary wife. The union is successful from a biological standpoint: Hagar conceives. However, the emotional and social dynamics within the camp shift dramatically. Empowered by her pregnancy—the very thing her mistress could not achieve—Hagar’s perspective changes. The scripture notes that “when she saw that she had conceived, she looked on her mistress with contempt.” This was more than mere pride; it was a deep, cutting scorn that undermined the entire social order and poured salt into Sarai’s deepest wound.

Sarai’s reaction is one of raw, furious hurt. She does not confront Hagar directly first; instead, she turns on Abram, the architect of the plan to which she had consented. Her words are a torrent of accusation and a call for divine justice: “May the wrong done to me be on you!” she cries. “I gave my servant to your embrace, and when she saw that she had conceived, she looked on me with contempt. May the LORD judge between you and me!” In her anguish, she holds Abram responsible for the breakdown of respect and the unbearable humiliation she now endures.

Abram, caught in the conflict, effectively returns authority to Sarai. His response, "Behold, your servant is in your power; do to her as you please," is a disengagement that grants Sarai full license to act. Empowered by this, Sarai "dealt harshly with her." The Hebrew term implies oppression and humiliation so severe that Hagar, despite the perils of the wilderness, chooses to flee. She becomes a runaway, pregnant and alone, heading back toward Egypt, her homeland.

But her flight is intercepted by divine grace. An angel of the LORD finds her by a spring of water in the desert. His first command is a difficult one: "Return to your mistress and submit to her." This was not an endorsement of Sarai's harsh treatment but a call to trust in a greater plan. Then, the angel delivers a profound prophecy, elevating Hagar's status from a despised pawn to the matriarch of a great nation. He tells her she will bear a son and must name him Ishmael (which means "God hears"), because the LORD has heard her affliction.

The prophecy for Ishmael is both a blessing and a sobering forecast: "He shall be a wild donkey of a man, his hand against everyone and everyone's hand against him, and he shall dwell over against all his kinsmen." Yet, crucially, the angel adds, "I will so greatly multiply your offspring that they cannot be numbered for multitude." This is a direct, breathtaking echo of the promise given to Abram in Chapter 12. Here, to an Egyptian slave girl in the desert, God reaffirms and begins to fulfill His covenant, demonstrating that His plans transcend human failings and social hierarchies.

Hagar, in response, gives a name to God Himself, calling Him El-Roi ("the God who sees me"), for she declares, "Truly here I have seen him who looks after me." Humbled and empowered by this divine encounter, she returns to Abram's camp and gives birth to Ishmael. Abram was eighty-six years old. This event sets the stage for the deep and enduring conflict that would follow, for Ishmael's birth precedes the birth of the promised son, Isaac, by fourteen years, creating a tangible and lasting tension between the son of the slave woman and the son of the free woman, a tension that echoes through history.

*****

Genesis chapter 17 represents a profound and pivotal turning point in the life of Sarai, a moment where her identity, destiny, and very body are redefined by divine promise after a long period of silence and seemingly barren hope. The chapter opens not in immediate action, but in a tense silence that has stretched for thirteen years since the tumultuous events surrounding the birth of Ishmael through her Egyptian maidservant, Hagar. This lengthy gap underscores a period of quiet stagnation, where Abram and Sarai may have assumed that God's promise had been fulfilled in Ishmael, settling into a reality that fell short of the original covenant.

The divine encounter that breaks this silence is monumental. "The Lord appeared to Abram" (Genesis 17:1), a phrasing that signifies a powerful and direct revelation. God establishes and formalizes the earlier covenant, but with crucial elaborations. He begins by revealing a new aspect of His own nature, instructing Abram to "walk before me faithfully and be blameless." This is not a distant God of mere promise, but one demanding a committed, ongoing relationship.

The core of the covenant is then restated and expanded: Abram is to be the father of many nations. To seal this transformed identity, God performs a profound act: He changes Abram's name to Abraham, meaning "father of a multitude." This is more than a new title; it is a prophetic declaration, speaking his future into his present identity. The promise of the land of Canaan is also reiterated as an "everlasting possession."

It is at this juncture that the narrative irrevocably shifts its focus to Sarai. After establishing the covenant with Abraham, God immediately turns the course of her life forever. In a parallel act of renaming that elevates her to an equal footing in the covenant, God changes her name from Sarai ("my princess") to Sarah ("princess" or "mother of nations"). This change signifies a shift from a possessive, individual status to a universal, dynastic one. God specifically blesses her, stating, "I will bless her and will surely give you a son by her." She is no longer a peripheral figure in the promise but is placed at its very center. The declaration that she will be a "mother of nations" and that "kings of peoples will come from her" is a staggering prophecy. This looks far beyond the immediate family, foreshadowing the rise of the Davidic monarchy and, ultimately, the lineage of the Messiah, Jesus Christ, who would come from the tribe of Judah, a descendant of Abraham and Sarah.

Faced with this impossible promise, Abraham's reaction is one of stark, human disbelief. He falls facedown in a posture of reverence, but his words are pure doubt. He laughs inwardly and argues with reality: "Will a son be born to a man a hundred years old? Will Sarah bear a child at the age of ninety?" His solution, born of pragmatic human reasoning rather than faith, is to suggest that God simply adopt Ishmael as the chosen heir: "If only Ishmael might live under your blessing!"

God's response is swift and unyielding. He does not entertain the compromise. The divine plan is specific and unalterable. The son will be born to Sarah, and his name will be Isaac, meaning "he laughs," a perpetual reminder of Abraham's momentary doubt and the joy that will replace it. It is with Isaac, God affirms, that He will establish His "everlasting covenant." Yet, in His immense grace, God does not dismiss Abraham's concern for his firstborn. While the covenant line will flow through Isaac, God hears the prayer for Ishmael. He promises to bless him, make him fruitful, and father twelve rulers—a promise that is later fulfilled and results in the formation of the Ishmaelite tribes, who are traditionally recognized in Islamic heritage as foundational figures.

The chapter concludes with the sign of this everlasting covenant: circumcision. Abraham, in a stunning display of immediate obedience despite the astounding news, gathers every male in his household. That very day, he and his son Ishmael (at thirteen years old, the exact age of the silence) and all the other men are circumcised. This physical mark sets them apart as the covenant people. Notably, the narrative closes with Sarah still unaware of the conversation that has just transpired. She remains in her tent, unknowingly on the precipice of a miracle, her future now secured by a divine decree that had yet to be spoken to her directly, setting the stage for the drama, laughter, and ultimate fulfillment that is to come.

*****

The eighteenth chapter of Genesis opens with a scene of profound tranquility and stark contrast. The patriarch Abraham is found at his home in the plains of Mamre, seeking respite from the oppressive, shimmering heat of the day. He rests at the opening of his tent, a position that signifies both authority and hospitality, offering a sliver of shade and a vantage point to see any travelers on the horizon. It is in this quiet moment that his solitude is interrupted by the appearance of three enigmatic men. The narrative reveals that one of these figures is none other than the LORD Himself, manifest in a tangible, approachable form, accompanied by two angelic attendants.

Demonstrating the esteemed Bedouin virtue of hospitality—a sacred duty in the harsh desert environment—Abraham does not wait for them to ask for assistance. He springs into action with urgent reverence. Rushing from his tent entrance, he bows low to the ground in a gesture of deep respect and deference. His offer is not merely polite; it is lavish and insistent. He pleads with the travelers not to pass by but to accept his ministrations: water to wash the dust from their feet, a place to rest beneath the shade of a nearby terebinth tree, and a "morsel of bread" to refresh themselves before they continue their journey.

This "morsel of bread," however, quickly transforms into a feast fit for an honored guest. Abraham's actions reveal the depth of his generosity. He hastens into the tent to Sarah and instructs her to quickly prepare three seahs of fine flour into cakes. This is a massive quantity—nearly two gallons of the finest, most expensive flour—indicating this is no simple snack but a significant undertaking. While this directive is given to Sarah, Abraham's role as the active host continues. He himself runs to his herd, selects a tender and choice calf, and gives it to a servant, who hurriedly prepares it. He then brings this lavish spread of curds, milk, and the freshly prepared veal to his guests and stands attentively near them under the tree as they eat, embodying the role of a servant to his divine visitors.

It is in the midst of this shared meal that the true purpose of the visit is unveiled. The visitors ask a pointed question: "Where is Sarah, your wife?" This is deeply significant, as it not only shows they know her name but also deliberately includes her in the conversation, shifting the narrative's focus to the promised heir. Abraham's simple reply, "There, in the tent," sets the stage for the divine pronouncement. The LORD then makes the unequivocal promise: "I will surely return to you about this time next year, and Sarah your wife will have a son."

Sarah, listening just inside the tent door, hidden from view yet central to the prophecy, overhears these words. Her immediate, visceral reaction is one of inward, skeptical laughter. She laughs to herself, a silent, private burst of incredulity. The text poignantly reveals her inner monologue: "After I am worn out, and my lord is old, shall I have pleasure?" Her laughter is not one of joy but of painful irony and decades of disappointed hope. She focuses on the physical impossibility—her own aged, barren body and

Abraham's advanced age—and in doing so, momentarily overlooks the identity of the One making the promise.

Yet, the narrative underscores a fundamental truth of divine omniscience: the Lord hears everything, including the silent laughter of a heart wrestling with doubt. The LORD immediately addresses Abraham, though His words are meant for the eavesdropping Sarah: "Why did Sarah laugh?... Is anything too hard for the LORD?" This divine rhetorical question shifts the focus from human limitation to divine power. He reiterates the promise, transforming it from a prediction into an immutable decree.

Filled with fear and shame at being discovered in her doubt, Sarah emerges and does what comes naturally: she denies it. "I did not laugh," she says, perhaps fearing the consequence of her irreverence. But the Lord, both just and merciful, offers a final, gentle correction that leaves no room for denial: "No, but you did laugh." This simple, firm rebuttal is not a condemnation but a penetrating affirmation of His knowledge of the deepest chambers of the human heart. With this exchange, Sarah's active role in the chapter concludes, leaving her—and the reader—with the staggering weight of a promise that hinges not on human capability, but solely on the flawless power and faithfulness of God. The stage is now set for the laughter of disbelief to be transformed into the joyous laughter of fulfillment with the birth of their son, Isaac, whose name means "he laughs."

*****

While we will soon return to Sarah's pivotal story in Genesis Chapter 20, a powerful and tragic interlude is unfolding in the nearby region of Sodom. This narrative serves as a sobering counterpoint to God's covenant with Abraham and introduces a lineage crucial to the broader biblical story.

The scene opens in the notoriously wicked city of Sodom, a place so synonymous with depravity that its name would echo through history as a byword for sin and divine judgment. Here resides Lot, the nephew of Abraham. Though he initially journeyed with his uncle from Ur, Lot chose to settle in the fertile Jordan Plain, pitching his tents near, and eventually within, the walls of Sodom—a decision that would have grave consequences for his family.

Moved by his righteous concern for his nephew and the potential innocence within the city, Abraham famously interceded with the Lord, bargaining for Sodom's survival. Though not even ten righteous people could be found, God honored Abraham's plea in part by sending two angelic messengers to Sodom with an urgent mission: to rescue Lot and his family before the city's imminent and total destruction.

The angels find Lot sitting at the city gate, a position indicating some stature, but his hospitality is immediately tested by the violent demands of the men of Sodom, highlighting the city's profound moral decay. After a harrowing night protecting their divine guests, the angels deliver their grave warning at dawn: the city is to be obliterated, and Lot must gather his family and flee immediately to the mountains without a backward glance.

What follows is a scene of agonizing hesitation. Lot's sons-in-law dismiss the warning as a joke, and even Lot himself lingers, seemingly paralyzed by the thought of abandoning his home and possessions. So great is the Lord's mercy that the angels physically seize Lot, his wife, and his two unmarried daughters and lead them out of the city, urging them to run for their lives and not to stop or look back upon the cataclysm.

As fiery sulfur rains down from heaven, consuming everything in its path, a profound human tragedy occurs. Lot's wife, who remains unnamed, perhaps symbolizing her representing a universal failing, cannot resist. Overcome by grief, nostalgia, or simple disbelief, she disobeys the angel's singular command. She turns and looks back upon the home she loved, and in that moment, she is transformed into a pillar of salt—a lasting monument to the peril of clinging to a sinful past and the cost of disobedience.

Now utterly alone save for his two daughters, a traumatized Lot finds the safety of the small town of Zoar insufficient and convinces himself to flee further into the mountains, where they take refuge in a desolate cave. It is in this stark and hopeless setting that a desperate plan is born. Believing themselves to be the last humans alive on a seemingly empty, scorched earth, Lot's daughters see no future for humanity. In a twisted act of preservation, they devise a scheme to continue their father's lineage. On two consecutive nights, they get their father drunk with wine to a point of unconsciousness, and each lies with him without his knowledge.

From these deeply fraught and morally complex unions, both daughters conceive sons. The older daughter gives birth to a son she names Moab, which sounds like the Hebrew for "from my father." The younger daughter names her son

Ben-Ammi, meaning “son of my people.” These boys become the forefathers of two significant nations: the Moabites and the Ammonites.

It is Moab who becomes a critical person of interest in the broader biblical narrative. As the father of the Moabites, he establishes the lineage of a people who would become frequent adversaries, and sometimes unlikely allies, of Israel. Most importantly, these Moabites are the people of Ruth, the revered Moabite woman whose story of loyalty and faith we will explore later. It is a profound irony of genealogy that Ruth, a Moabite, and thus a descendant of Lot’s firstborn daughter, would marry into the nation of Israel (the Hebrews, descendants of her great-uncle Abraham). This makes Ruth, though ethnically Moabite, a genetic descendant of the original Hebrew family through her ancestor Lot. She would ultimately become the great-grandmother of King David and thus a direct ancestor in the earthly lineage of Jesus Christ.

This dark detour through the ashes of Sodom thus establishes a crucial thread in the tapestry of redemption. From the depths of depravity, judgment, and human frailty emerges a lineage that, generations later, would be woven directly into the story of the Messiah. With this connection established, the narrative now turns its focus back to Sarah and the next chapter in the story of God’s promise.

*****

The narrative in Genesis 20 presents a profound and unsettling echo of a story from Abraham's past, challenging the reader to understand the continued fragility of the patriarch's faith even after decades of God's promises. The scene opens with Abraham's decision to sojourn in the southern region of Gerar, a Philistine kingdom. Despite being the recipient of a divine covenant and the specific promise that a great nation would descend from him and Sarah, a familiar fear grips Abraham. Worried that the local king, Abimelech, might kill him to take his beautiful wife, Abraham consciously reverted to the same half-truth he had employed decades earlier in Egypt (Genesis 12): he introduced Sarah, his wife, as his sister.

This deliberate deception set a tragicomedy of errors into motion. As Abraham had cynically predicted, King Abimelech, believing Sarah to be an eligible, unmarried woman, had her brought into his household, likely as a preliminary step toward making her his wife. However, the dynamic of this story sharply diverges from the Egyptian episode. Here, God Himself intervenes directly before any irreparable harm is done. He appears to the unsuspecting Abimelech in a dream—a common biblical method of divine communication with non-Israelites—and delivers a terrifying pronouncement: "Behold, you are a dead man because of the woman whom you have taken, for she is a man's wife."

Confronted with his unwitting transgression, Abimelech responds not with defiance, but with a passionate and reasoned plea of innocence that stands in stark contrast to Abraham's deception. He appeals to God's own sense of justice, arguing, "Lord, will You slay a righteous nation also?" His defense is threefold: he acted on the information given to him by both Abraham and Sarah ("Did he not say to me, 'She is my sister'? And she, even she herself said, 'He is my brother'"), and, most importantly, he acted with pure motives

("In the integrity of my heart and innocence of my hands I have done this").

In a powerful demonstration of divine justice that distinguishes between intentional sin and unintentional error, God acknowledges the validity of Abimelech's plea. He reveals that it was His own restraining hand that prevented the king from touching Sarah, thus preserving Abimelech from committing a mortal sin. Yet, a consequence for the royal house had already been enacted: God had "closed all the wombs" of the women in Abimelech's household, a direct affliction on the source of life and legacy for the kingdom, mirroring the threat to the promise held within Sarah.

God then issues a clear command: Abimelech must restore Sarah to Abraham. The reason given is crucial and reveals Abraham's elevated status: he is a prophet. This is the first time this title is used in the Bible, and it comes with a responsibility. As a mediator between God and man, Abraham is instructed to pray for Abimelech, for only his intercession can reverse the divinely imposed barrenness and avert the death of the king and his people.

The next morning, Abimelech acts with urgent obedience. He summons Abraham and confronts him with a question that hangs heavy with accusation and confusion: "What have you done to us? And how have I offended you, that you have brought on me and on my kingdom a great sin?" Abraham's response is a revealing glimpse into his fear and flawed logic. He explains that he assumed there was "no fear of God" in Gerar and that he would be killed for his wife. He then rationalizes his lie with a technicality: Sarah is, in fact, his half-sister, the daughter of his father but not his mother.

While perhaps factually true, it was a deliberate obfuscation of the more significant truth of their marital covenant.

In a stunning act of grace and restitution, the wronged king does not punish the patriarch. Instead, Abimelech abundantly restores Sarah to Abraham, compounding his apology with a lavish gift meant to publicly vindicate her honor and compensate the couple: sheep, oxen, and male and female servants to attest to their renewed wealth and status. Most significantly, he gives Abraham a thousand pieces of silver, which he declares is to be for Sarah—a "covering of the eyes" for all who are with her, a symbolic payment that officially clears any suspicion of guilt from her and re-establishes her dignity before the entire community.

The chapter concludes with the fulfillment of God's directive. Abraham, the prophet, prayed to God on behalf of Abimelech. In response to this intercession, God healed the king and his household, opening the wombs of the women that He had closed. Thus, life and fertility were restored to Gerar, all stemming from the prayer of the very man whose deception had threatened to destroy it. The story ends by highlighting a profound theme: God's protection of His covenant promise, even through the imperfect actions of His chosen ones, and His mercy that extends to righteous Gentiles who seek Him in integrity.

*****

Genesis Chapter 21 opens with the long-awaited and miraculous culmination of a divine covenant—the birth of Isaac. This event was not a mere biological surprise; it was the precise fulfillment of a decades-old promise God had made to Abraham and Sarah, a promise they had often doubted and even laughed at in their old age. The scripture emphasizes the specificity of God's timing, noting that Isaac was born "at the set time of which God had spoken," a testament to the Lord's faithfulness even when human hope seems exhausted.

Sarah, whose years of barrenness had been a source of deep pain and social shame, is now utterly transformed by joy. The laughter of disbelief that once greeted the angel's prophecy is replaced with the laughter of pure, ecstatic delight. She declares, "God has made me laugh, and all who hear will laugh with me." For a time, Abraham's household is a place of perfect harmony and celebration, basking in the fulfillment of God's word.

This peace, however, is fractured on the day of Isaac's weaning, a significant milestone in the ancient world marking a child's survival past infancy. To honor this moment, Abraham throws a great feast. Amid the celebrations, Sarah's keen eyes observe Ishmael, Abraham's firstborn son by her Egyptian maidservant, Hagar. The text says Ishmael was "scoffing" or "mocking." While the exact nature of his actions is debated, the context suggests it was more than childish play; it was likely an act of derision or jealous provocation directed at the younger Isaac, the heir who had displaced his position.

Fueled by a mother's fierce protectiveness over her son's divine inheritance, Sarah makes a drastic and harsh demand. She insists that Abraham permanently expel Hagar and Ishmael from their camp. Her reasoning is starkly practical and political: "Cast out this bondwoman and her son; for the son of this bondwoman shall not be heir with my son, Isaac." This was not merely about a single incident; it was about securing Isaac's sole claim to the covenant promises of God and the vast wealth of Abraham.

The demand devastated Abraham. Ishmael was his son, a boy he had loved and raised for over a decade. The thought of casting him and his mother out into the perilous wilderness was deeply grievous to him. Torn between his love for his firstborn and the demands of his wife, Abraham sought divine counsel.

In His infinite mercy, God intervened to comfort and guide the patriarch. He instructed Abraham, "Do not let it be displeasing in your sight because of the lad or because of your bondwoman. Whatever Sarah has said to you, listen to her voice; for in Isaac your seed shall be called. Yet I will also make a nation of the son of the bondwoman, because he is your seed." This profound statement affirmed that God's primary covenant lineage would indeed flow through Isaac, yet it also held a magnificent promise for Ishmael. He, too, as a son of Abraham, would be under God's providential care and would become the father of a great nation. Assured of this, Abraham obeyed.

The next morning, with a heavy heart, Abraham provided Hagar and the young boy with provisions—a skin of water and some bread—and sent them away into the wilderness of Beersheba. Their supplies, meager against the harsh environment, soon ran out. Overcome by heat, thirst, and despair, Hagar could not bear to watch her child die. She placed Ishmael under the shade of a shrub and walked a distance away, weeping in resignation.

But God, who had heard the laughter of Sarah, now heard the desperate cries of the boy. In a moment of divine compassion, the angel of God called out to Hagar from heaven, saying, "What ails you, Hagar? Fear not, for God has heard the voice of the lad where he is. Arise, lift up the lad and hold him with your hand, for I will make him a great nation." This reassurance mirrored the promise given to Abraham, making Hagar the first person in scripture to receive a divine annunciation twice.

Then, God opened Hagar's eyes. Where she had seen only certain death, she now saw a well of life-giving water. She hurried to fill the skin and gave her dying son a drink. The narrative concludes with a summary of their divinely guided future: "God was with the lad; and he grew." He became a skilled archer, making a life for himself in the wilderness of Paran. In a poignant full-circle moment, his mother, Hagar the Egyptian, secured a wife for him from her homeland of Egypt.

This concludes the direct biblical narrative of Hagar, a woman whose life was marked by hardship, divine encounter, and ultimate redemption. Though she exits the stage, her lineage, the Ishmaelites, re-enters the grand biblical story later when her descendants become the agents of another pivotal event: they are the traders who purchase Joseph from his brothers and take him to Egypt, setting in motion the events that would lead to the salvation of the nation of Israel.

*****

The twenty-second chapter of Genesis presents one of the most profound and harrowing narratives in all of scripture: the Akedah, or the binding of Isaac. This story details God's ultimate test of Abraham's faith, commanding him to sacrifice his long-awaited son, the child of the promise, on Mount Moriah. The text meticulously chronicles Abraham's obedient journey, the heart-wrenching dialogue with his unsuspecting son—"God himself will provide the lamb for the burnt offering, my son"—and the divine intervention at the final moment, where a ram is provided as a substitute. The story concludes with God reaffirming His covenant with Abraham, blessing him for his unwavering faithfulness.

Yet, this monumental narrative is marked by a profound and haunting silence: the complete absence of Sarah, Isaac's mother. Scripture provides no account of her knowledge, her fears, or her anguish. We are left to wonder: did Abraham tell her of God's command as he gathered the wood and the knife? Or did he depart quietly, leaving her with a father's lie about a journey of worship? The text offers no clue, leaving a vacuum of maternal perspective at the heart of this foundational story of faith and sacrifice.

Tragically, we never learn of Sarah's reaction because her story concludes immediately afterward. The very next chapter, Genesis 23, opens with the stark announcement of her death at the age of 127 years. This abrupt transition is deeply significant. The rabbinic midrash and centuries of theological reflection have often filled this silence with poignant speculation. Some traditions suggest that the shock of hearing about her son's near-sacrifice—whether from a divine messenger, a distraught Isaac, or a grieving Abraham—was the catalyst that ended her life. Her story, which began with laughter at the promise of Isaac's birth ("Isaac" means "he laughs"), ends in the silence of the grave.

The narrative then shifts from the theological test on the mountain to a practical, solemn transaction on the ground. In a moving act of grief and love, Abraham, " mourning and weeping for Sarah," seeks a permanent burial place for his wife. As a sojourner in the land promised to his descendants, he owns no part of it. He therefore approaches the sons of Heth in Hebron and, with great humility and persistence, negotiates to purchase the field of Machpelah, with its cave at the end of the field. The negotiation is a formal, public ceremony, and Abraham insists on paying the full market price to secure an indisputable claim. The sum, 400 shekels of silver, is weighed out and accepted, making the cave and the field Abraham's legal property.

This acquisition is far more than a simple real estate deal; it is an act of profound faith. With this purchase, Abraham, the wanderer, takes the first tangible, permanent foothold in the Promised Land. The field of Machpelah becomes the burial place for the patriarchs and matriarchs—Sarah, and eventually Abraham, Isaac, Rebekah, Leah, and Jacob. It is the seed of the inheritance God swore to give his people. Thus, the narrative arc moves from the agony of a potential loss on Moriah to the secure, legally-grounded resting place in Machpelah, anchoring the future of the covenant in the very dust of the land from which Sarah, and all who followed, were formed.

Before moving forward from this pivotal section of Genesis, it is essential to pause and reflect on the profound, divinely orchestrated connection between the three maternal figures we have encountered: Hagar, Lot's eldest daughter, and Sarah. Each gave birth to a lineage that would become a nation, and their stories are intricately woven into the fabric of salvation history.

Hagar, the Egyptian maidservant, bore Ishmael, whose descendants became the Ishmaelites, a nomadic trading people of the desert. Lot's eldest daughter, in a desperate act to preserve her father's line after the destruction of Sodom, bore Moab, the progenitor of the Moabites, a people who settled east of the Dead Sea. Sarah, the matriarch of the promise, bore Isaac, the child of the covenant, through whom God's chosen line would continue. The subsequent intersections of these three lines are nothing short of miraculous.

The Ishmaelites, acting as agents of divine providence, were the traders to whom Joseph's brothers sold him into slavery in Egypt (Genesis 37:28). Had this heartbreaking betrayal not occurred—facilitated by Abraham's other son—Joseph would never have risen to power in Egypt, been in a position to save the known world from famine, or ultimately rescued his own family, the fledgling nation of Israel. Without this sojourn in Egypt, Israel's development as a distinct nation, its Exodus, and its reception of the Law at Sinai would never have happened. The entire future of the people of God hung on this single act by the Ishmaelites.

The modern implications of this ancient event are staggering to consider. Had Israel's history ended early, the world would be irrevocably impoverished. The descendants of Isaac, the Jewish people, have contributed immeasurably to human civilization. In the field of medicine alone, we would be without the polio vaccine (developed by Jonas Salk), the ingestible pill camera (Given Imaging), and foundational research leading to treatments for countless diseases. Beyond medicine, Israeli innovation has gifted the world with ubiquitous technologies like the USB flash drive (DiskOnKey), cellphone technology (with major developments from companies like Motorola Israel), and even beloved cultural touchstones like the instant camera (developed by Edwin Land, inspired by an idea from his daughter) and candies like Mike and Ike. Their contributions have indeed made global life healthier, more convenient, and more enjoyable.

Yet, the divine tapestry woven from these three women's lines does not end there. We must also give thanks to God, whose sovereign plan incorporated even the Moabites. For it was from that very nation—born from Lot's daughter—that a young woman named Ruth would emerge. Her faithful love for her Israelite mother-in-law and her conversion to faith in the God of Israel led her to Bethlehem, where she would marry Boaz. From their union would come Obed, then Jesse, and then David, the great king of Israel, the Lion of the tribe of Judah. This royal lineage, infused with Moabite blood, would continue down through the generations, fulfilling the prophecy that from Judah would come an eternal ruler. Thus, the ultimate Lion of Judah, Jesus Christ, would centuries later be born from the womb of a young Jewish woman, Mary, a direct descendant of this very line—a story we will explore in much greater depth later.

In this breathtaking way, the strands of Hagar, Lot's daughter, and Sarah all converge in the grand narrative of redemption.

The Matriarch of two nations: Rebekah

Our journey through the Scriptures to meet the foundational women of the faith now brings us to a pivotal and beautifully detailed narrative in Genesis 24. Here, we are introduced to Rebekah, a woman whose character and decisive actions would forever shape the destiny of the Israelite nation. Her story is not one of chance, but a meticulously orchestrated divine appointment, demonstrating God's profound faithfulness to His covenant with Abraham.

The stage is set three years after the death of Sarah. The patriarch Abraham, now old and well-advanced in years, is burdened with a sacred concern: securing a worthy wife for his son Isaac, the child of promise. The surrounding Canaanite culture, with its pagan deities and practices, was unsuitable for the heir through whom God's covenant would be established. Driven by faith, Abraham summons his most trusted servant—likely Eliezer of Damascus mentioned earlier (Gen. 15:2)—and charges him with a solemn oath. This was no mere errand; it was a sacred mission. Abraham made the servant swear he would not choose a Canaanite woman for Isaac but would instead journey back to Abraham's homeland and kin in Mesopotamia to find a suitable wife.

Crucially, Abraham also insisted that Isaac himself must not go. The heir of the promise could not leave the land God had sworn to give his descendants; the promise must come to him. Demonstrating remarkable faith, Abraham assured his servant that God would send His angel ahead to prepare the way and ensure the mission's success. In an act of great wisdom and fairness, Abraham also released the servant from the oath if the chosen woman was unwilling to leave her homeland, showing that God's plan would not be forced upon an unwilling heart.

The narrative then shifts to the servant's point of view, chronicling his journey of faith. He took ten of his master's camels—a sign of immense wealth and a generous bridal party—and made the long, arduous trek north to the city of Nahor in Aram-naharaim (Mesopotamia). Upon arrival, he strategically positioned his camels at the central well just outside the city during the evening, the precise time when young women would traditionally gather to draw water.

Here, the servant demonstrates his own profound faith. Rather than devising a complex strategy, he prays directly to the "LORD, God of my master Abraham." He petitions God for chesed—covenant loyalty and kindness—and proposes a specific, gracious sign to identify the right woman. His test was not based on superficiality but on character: the woman who would not only offer him a drink from her heavy jar but would also, on her own initiative, offer to water his ten thirsty camels would be the one. This was no small offer; watering ten camels after a long desert journey could involve drawing up to 250 gallons of water—a task requiring immense physical strength, a generous spirit, and remarkable hospitality.

Astonishingly, the divine response was immediate. Before he had finished praying, Rebekah arrived at the well. The text is careful to note she was the daughter of Bethuel, who was the son of Nahor (Abraham's brother) and his wife Milcah. She was not only born into the right family but was also "very beautiful to behold, a virgin; no man had known her." The servant watched, likely holding his breath, as she filled her pitcher. When he asked for a drink, she quickly and kindly obliged. Then, exceeding all expectations, she proactively declared, "I will draw water for your camels also, until they have finished drinking." She tirelessly worked until the enormous task was complete.

Overwhelmed with awe, the servant witnessed his precise prayer being fulfilled before his eyes. He immediately worshiped, declaring, "Blessed be the LORD, the God of my master Abraham, who has not forsaken His kindness and His truth toward my master!" He bestowed upon her lavish gifts of gold, inquired of her lineage, and discovered she was his master's own great-niece. In reverence, he bowed his head and worshipped God again for His direct guidance.

The chapter concludes with Rebekah's courageous decision. After hearing the servant's full story of the divine encounter, and when asked, "Will you go with this man?" She did not hesitate. With a faith that mirrored Abraham's own call to leave his homeland, she simply replied, "I will go." Her agreement to depart immediately sealed her destiny. She left her family to journey to a land she had never seen, to marry a man she had never met, trusting in the God who had so clearly ordained her path. In doing so, Rebekah, the kind and strong-willed woman at the well, became the second matriarch of Israel.

*****

Following the pivotal story of Isaac and Rebekah's divinely orchestrated marriage, Genesis Chapter 25 provides a crucial interlude, tying up the narrative of the patriarch Abraham before fully transitioning the focus to the next generation. The chapter opens with a brief but significant detour, informing us that Abraham took another wife after Sarah's death, a woman named Keturah. Though some traditions suggest she may have been a concubine or secondary wife earlier in his life, the text presents this union as a late chapter in Abraham's life. With Keturah, Abraham fathered six sons: Zimran, Jokshan, Medan, Midian, Ishbak, and Shuah. These sons became the progenitors of various Arabian tribes, establishing Abraham as not just the father of one nation, but a literal "father of many nations" as God had promised. However, in a decisive act that secures the covenant lineage, Abraham distinguishes his heirs. While he gave gifts to the sons of Keturah and sent them away eastward to ensure no challenge to the chosen heir, he bestowed his entire inheritance—all his wealth, rights, and, most importantly, the covenant blessings of God—exclusively upon his son Isaac.

The narrative then solemnly records the death of the great patriarch, Abraham, at the venerable age of 175 years. In a moment of poignant reconciliation, his two sons, Isaac and Ishmael, who had been separated by decades of strife and exile, came together to bury their father. They laid him to rest in the cave of Machpelah alongside his beloved first wife, Sarah, reuniting them in death. This act of shared filial duty offers a brief, peaceful resolution to their fractured history. Following this, the text formally concludes Ishmael's story, chronicling his descendants—twelve tribal rulers—and noting his death at 137 years old, his legacy living on as God's promise to make him a great nation was fulfilled.

The focus of the sacred history then narrows sharply onto the line of Isaac. We learn that Isaac was forty years old when he married Rebekah, echoing the patient waiting that characterized his parents' story. Yet, this echo extended to a painful reality: like her mother-in-law Sarah before her, Rebekah was barren. For twenty years, the couple remained childless, a period of anguish and testing of their faith. In a powerful demonstration of supplication, Isaac, unlike his father who took matters into his own hands with Hagar, pleaded directly with the Lord on behalf of his wife. In response to his faithful entreaty, God granted his plea, and Rebekah conceived.

Her pregnancy, however, was fraught with difficulty. The children struggled violently within her womb, a conflict so severe that Rebekah despairingly wondered aloud if there was any purpose to her life if this was her experience. In her distress, she went to inquire of the Lord. God's response was not a remedy for her physical discomfort but a profound revelation that framed the entire future of Israel's history. He told her, "Two nations are in your womb, and two peoples from within you will be separated; one people will be stronger than the other, and the older will serve the younger." This divine oracle established the spiritual primacy of the younger son over the firstborn, subverting ancient cultural conventions and highlighting that God's election operates on a different principle than human tradition.

When the time came, Rebekah indeed gave birth to twin boys. Their entry into the world vividly foreshadowed their contrasting natures and future conflict. The firstborn was red and covered in hair like a rough garment; they named him Esau, meaning "hairy" or "red." The second son emerged grasping his brother's heel, an act of relentless pursuit from the very beginning; he was named Jacob, meaning "he grasps the heel" or, figuratively, "he supplants." As they grew, their parents developed clear favorites, a familial dynamic that would fuel future deception and heartbreak. Isaac loved Esau, the rugged outdoorsman and skilled hunter who provided him with wild game. Rebekah loved Jacob, the quiet man who dwelt in tents. This preference was not necessarily a matter of neglecting the other son, but it created a dangerous schism in the family. Rebekah's partiality was likely deeply intertwined with the divine prophecy she had received; she loved Jacob not just as a son, but as the bearer of God's mysterious promise.

The chapter concludes with a defining incident that encapsulates the characters of the twins and the nature of the transferred birthright. Returning from the field one day, exhausted and famished, the impulsive Esau found Jacob preparing a hearty red stew. Driven by immediate physical need and showing contempt for his spiritual inheritance, Esau agreed to sell his invaluable birthright—his status as firstborn, which entitled him to a double portion of the inheritance and the covenant leadership of the family—to his cunning younger brother in exchange for a single meal of bread and lentil stew. With a dramatic oath, he finalized the trade, and Jacob, ever the opportunist, secured the prize for the price of a bowl of stew. This transaction, though seemingly opportunistic, was divinely situated, demonstrating how Esau's own worldly disposition led him to forfeit the promise, setting the stage for the tumultuous chapters to follow.

*****

In a stark echo of his father's past, the narrative of Chapter 26 opens with a familiar and devastating crisis: a severe famine grips the land of Canaan. Faced with this existential threat, Isaac, the son of the promise, makes a decision reminiscent of Abraham's journey generations before. He sets his course for Gerar, seeking refuge in the territory of Abimelech, king of the Philistines. This decision, however, was not born solely of human instinct. Prior to his journey, God had appeared to Isaac with a specific and restrictive command: he was not to follow the well-trodden path down to Egypt, the perennial breadbasket in times of trouble. Instead, he was instructed to remain as a sojourner in the land that God would designate for him—a test of faith that required trusting divine provision over the obvious, human solution.

To fortify Isaac for this challenge, God then solemnly reiterated the foundational covenant promises originally made to Abraham. He swore to be with Isaac, to bless him, to give all these lands to his descendants, and to multiply his offspring until they became as countless as the stars. This powerful theophany was meant to be the bedrock of Isaac's courage. Yet, upon arriving in the politically volatile city of Gerar, fear rapidly eroded his faith. Isaac, the bearer of God's cosmic promise, succumbed to a very human anxiety. Looking upon his wife, Rebekah, whose beauty was renowned, he grew terrified that the men of the place would kill him to take her. In a moment of weak imitation, he pulled a page directly from his father's flawed playbook: he presented Rebekah to the community not as his wife, but merely as his sister.

There was, however, a critical moral distinction between the two deceptions. When Abraham had employed this ruse with Sarah, it was a half-truth, as she was indeed his half-sister. Isaac's claim held no such veneer of legitimacy; Rebekah was his first cousin once removed, making the lie far more blatant. For a time, the façade held. But the truth was inevitably revealed when the ever-watchful King Abimelech peered from his window and witnessed Isaac and Rebekah together in a moment of intimate endearment—a display of affection clearly reserved for a husband and wife, not a brother and sister. Summoning Isaac, Abimelech confronted him with a pointed and accusatory question: "What is this you have done to us? One of the men might easily have lain with your wife, and you would have brought guilt upon us and our kingdom." Isaac, exposed and ashamed, confessed his motive was sheer fright for his own life. While Abimelech's primary concern seemed to be avoiding divine retribution for unintended transgression, he nonetheless issued a royal decree, a public proclamation protecting Rebekah and threatening death to any man who dared to touch her.

God's blessing upon Isaac, as promised, proved to be exponentially fruitful. He sowed crops in that inhospitable land and reaped a hundredfold harvest that very year. His flocks and herds multiplied prodigiously, and he amassed a great number of servants. His prosperity became so immense and visibly overwhelming that he incurred the bitter envy of the Philistines, who began to stop up the wells his father had dug. Finally, an envious and threatened Abimelech was forced to admit Isaac's inherent power, telling him, "Go away from us, for you have become much mightier than we are." Forced to relocate, Isaac eventually settled in the Valley of Gerar and later moved to Beersheba, where God appeared to him again, confirming the covenant and compelling Isaac to build an altar and call upon the name of the Lord.

It is in this new home in Beersheba that the story turns to Rebekah, revealing a deep-seated bitterness in her personal life that paralleled the public conflicts her husband faced. Their son Esau, in defiance of his parents' spiritual heritage and likely seeking political alliances, had married two Hittite women: Judith and Basemath. These marriages were a source of profound grief and misery for both Isaac and Rebekah. The text specifies that the women were "a bitterness of spirit" to them, primarily because they were idolatrous, clinging to the pagan Canaanite practices that stood in direct opposition to the covenant faith of Isaac's family. For Rebekah, this alienation was almost certainly compounded by a deep-seated ethnic and cultural aversion. The Hittites were descended from Heth, a son of Canaan, who was himself a grandson of Ham—the son Noah had cursed. To Rebekah, these women were not just irksome daughters-in-law; they represented the very "people of the land" whose practices Abraham had zealously avoided and whose influence now threatened to corrupt the chosen family line from within.

*****

Genesis Chapter 27 stands as a profound and tragic turning point, marking the end of Rebekah's active and influential presence in the biblical narrative. The chapter is a masterclass in dramatic irony and familial dysfunction, where the seeds of favoritism sown years earlier (Genesis 25:28) erupt into a full-blown crisis of deception and stolen destiny.

The scene opens with a poignant image: the patriarch Isaac, now ancient and frail, his eyesight dimmed to near blindness. This physical vulnerability becomes the catalyst for the ensuing drama. Sensing his mortality, he summons his eldest son, Esau, the rugged outdoorsman. In a moment of touching, very human desire, Isaac asks Esau to hunt wild game and prepare the "savory food" he loves—a final meal that would serve as the prelude to the solemn, irrevocable act of bestowing the patriarchal blessing. This blessing was far more than a well-wish; it was a legal bequest of the birthright, conveying the covenant promises made to Abraham, including leadership of the family and the divine pledge of land, descendants, and grace.

However, the tent walls are thin. Rebekah, who has always favored Jacob, overhears the conversation. Fearing that God's earlier oracle ("the older shall serve the younger") would be thwarted by her husband's traditional instincts, she springs into action. Rather than confronting Isaac or appealing to God in prayer, she devises a complex and deceitful plan to secure the blessing for her favored son. She instructs Jacob to fetch two choice young goats from the flock, which she will prepare to mimic the savory dish Isaac expects from Esau.

Jacob's response reveals not a moral objection to the deception itself, but a practical fear of its failure and the dire consequences. He points out the obvious flaw: Esau is a hairy man, while his own skin is smooth. The difference is not merely cosmetic; it would be the primary means by which the blind Isaac would verify his son's identity. Rebekah's response is one of the most startling moments in the story. She demonstrates a fierce, almost ruthless, determination, absorbing all potential risk: "Let your curse be upon me, my son," she says. "Only obey my voice." This statement highlights her absolute conviction in her plan and her willingness to bear the divine wrath, if any, to ensure Jacob's success.

With her son's compliance secured, Rebekah executes her plan with meticulous detail. She prepares the food. Then, she engages in a symbolic act of disguise: she dresses Jacob in Esau's best clothes, ensuring he carries the scent of the field and his brother. To simulate Esau's hairiness, she takes the skins of the slaughtered kids and binds them to Jacob's hands and the smooth part of his neck.

The encounter between the disguised Jacob and his blind father is fraught with tension and psychological complexity. Isaac, though blind, is not fooled easily. He is immediately suspicious. "Who are you, my son?" he asks. When Jacob boldly claims, "I am Esau, your firstborn," Isaac's senses conflict. He calls him closer. He feels the goat skins and acknowledges, "The hands are the hands of Esau." But his hearing tells a different story: "The voice is the voice of Jacob."

This famous line is deeply insightful. It suggests that while the physical disguise was convincing, the inner character could not be fully hidden. Jacob's manner of speech—perhaps his tone, his vocabulary, his inflection—betrayed his thoughtful, domestic nature, which stood in stark contrast to Esau's rougher demeanor. It implies a spiritual difference as well; Jacob, the "dweller in tents," may have spoken of God with more intimacy and respect than his brother, whose priorities lay elsewhere. After a third, tense question, Isaac is finally convinced by the combined evidence of the smell of the fields on the clothes and the feel of the goat hair. He partakes of the meal and, in a moment of immense consequence, pronounces the full blessing of the firstborn upon Jacob, transferring the wealth and authority of the Abrahamic covenant to him.

The dramatic irony peaks moments after Jacob's departure. Esau arrives, fresh from the hunt, with his own prepared savory food, eager to receive his blessing. The revelation of what has transpired is devastating. Isaac trembles violently, realizing he has been deceived and that his solemn blessing, once given, cannot be rescinded or transferred. Esau erupts in a raw, painful cry of betrayal and anguish, "Bless me, even me also, O my father!"... "Have you not reserved a blessing for me?" His bitter lament, "Is he not rightly named Jacob? For he has supplanted me these two times," ties the act directly to the meaning of Jacob's name: "he grasps the heel" or "he supplants."

Facing Esau's murderous wrath, Rebekah is forced to send her beloved Jacob away to her brother Laban in Haran, under the pretext of finding a wife not from the local Hittite women—a concern she genuinely shared with Isaac. Her parting words, "Why should I be bereft of you both in one day?" reveal her fear of losing Jacob to murder and Esau to the law or his own rage. This departure, intended to last "a few days," stretched into twenty years. Scripture provides no record of a reunion between Rebekah and Jacob. She passes from the active narrative, her story concluding not with a final deed or word, but with her absence. We learn later that she was buried in the cave of Machpelah alongside Isaac, Abraham, and Sarah, a matriarch who shaped destiny through both faith and deeply flawed human cunning.

The Matriarchs of the 12 Tribes: Leah and Rachel

While our study of the women of the Word has thus far followed a singular focus, this next section will introduce a pivotal shift: we will be examining the lives and roles of two women simultaneously. Their intertwined stories form a complex tapestry of love, rivalry, and ultimately, the building of the nation of Israel.

However, before we delve into the rich narrative of Genesis chapter 29 and the stories of Leah and Rachel, it is prudent to pause and briefly consider the concluding verses of the preceding chapter. Genesis 28 provides a crucial piece of context that highlights the ongoing turmoil within Isaac's family. We find that Esau, in a belated and strategic effort to regain the favor of his parents, Isaac and Rebekah, after losing his birthright and blessing to Jacob, takes a decisive action. He takes a third wife. In a deliberate move away from his previous choices, which had been a source of grief for his parents (Genesis 26:34-35), this new wife is not a Hittite from the local Canaanite peoples. Instead, he marries Mahalath, the daughter of Ishmael—making her an Ishmaelite and thus a descendant of Abraham, albeit through the line of the slave woman, Hagar.

Esau's primary motivation for this union was a calculated attempt to finally secure some form of blessing and approval from his father, Isaac, by aligning himself more closely with the Abrahamic lineage. Despite this political maneuver, the text implies it was too little, too late to change his established fate. From this marriage, the descendants of Esau and Mahalath, combined with his other lines, would go on to form the nation known as the Edomites. This stands as yet another fulfillment of God's promise to Abraham that he would be the father of many nations (Genesis 17:4-5), a legacy that extended beyond the chosen line of Isaac and Jacob to include the Ishmaelites, the Edomites, and others through his concubines. This broader perspective sets the stage for understanding how the specific story of Jacob's family in chapter 29 fits into the grand, unfolding plan of redemption.

*****

We now transition into the pivotal and deeply consequential narrative of Chapter 29, which marks a significant turning point in the story of Jacob. Having fled from the justified wrath of his brother, Esau, and received the divine promise at Bethel, Jacob's long and arduous journey culminates as he finally arrives in the land of Haran, the homeland of his mother, Rebekah.

His arrival is marked by a scene of pastoral routine that is rich with symbolic foreshadowing. At a central well in the fields, its mouth sealed by a large stone—a communal safeguard—Jacob encounters a group of local shepherds waiting to water their flocks. In this seemingly mundane exchange, the wheels of destiny begin to turn. Jacob inquires if they know his uncle, Laban, the son of Nahor. They confirm they do, and remarkably, at that very moment, they point out that Laban's daughter, Rachel, is approaching with her father's sheep.

This introduction is significant, as it presents us with scripture's first named shepherdess—a role that denotes responsibility and strength. (We will encounter another pivotal shepherdess, Zipporah, in the Book of Exodus.) Witnessing Rachel's arrival, a profound and impulsive act of kinship and strength unfolds. Moved by a surge of emotion and perhaps a desire to prove his worth, Jacob single-handedly rolls the heavy stone from the well's mouth, an act typically requiring multiple men. He then waters the flock of Laban, his uncle. Overwhelmed—by the fulfillment of his journey, the memory of his mother (Rachel's aunt), and the striking presence of his cousin—Jacob weeps openly. He then kisses Rachel (a familial greeting, not yet romantic) and identifies himself as her kin, Rebekah's son. Rachel, in turn, hastily returns to her father to announce the stranger's arrival, and Laban himself comes out to warmly welcome his sister's son, inviting him into his household.

The narrative then carefully establishes the familial dynamics. For clarity, Laban is Rebekah's brother, making his daughters, Leah and Rachel, Jacob's first cousins. After Jacob had stayed for a month, contributing to the household's work, Laban, ever the shrewd negotiator, proposed a formal arrangement. He states, "Just because you are my relative does not mean you should work for me for nothing. Tell me what your wages should be."

It is at this contractual juncture that the text formally introduces Laban's two daughters, drawing a clear and consequential contrast between them. Leah is described as having "delicate eyes" (Hebrew rakkot), which may imply they were soft, tender, or perhaps weak—a descriptor that falls short of the era's standards of beauty. Rachel, however, is presented in radiant terms: she was "beautiful of form and appearance," a phrase echoing the description of legendary beauties like Sarah and Rebekah. Smitten, Jacob's choice is immediate and absolute. He offers an astonishing bride-price: seven years of labor for Rachel's hand in marriage. Laban readily agrees, and Jacob fulfills his term. The text poignantly notes that these seven years "seemed like only a few days to him because of his love for her."

When the agreed period concludes, Jacob rightfully demands his bride. Laban hosts a grand wedding feast, but under the cover of the celebrations and the dark of night, he executes a profound deception. In a cruel irony, the deceiver who stole his brother's blessing is now himself deceived. Laban substitutes Leah for Rachel in the marriage bed and gives Leah his maid, Zilpah, as her personal servant.

At dawn, the shocking revelation sends Jacob into a furious confrontation: "What is this you have done to me? Was it not for Rachel that I served you? Why have you deceived me?!" Laban's response is cool and calculated, cloaked in the rigid guise of local custom: "It is not so done in our place, to give the younger before the firstborn." His statement is dripping with irony, as he uses the principle of primogeniture—the very right Jacob had stolen from his firstborn brother—to defraud him. Laban proposes a solution: complete the bridal week with Leah, and then he may also marry Rachel in exchange for another seven years of labor. Trapped by his love for Rachel and the cultural reality of the consummated marriage to Leah, Jacob agrees. After the week, he marries Rachel, and Laban gives her his maid Bilhah as her servant.

The chapter closes on a note of poignant struggle and foundational beginnings. Like her foremothers Sarah and Rebekah, Rachel is barren, setting the stage for a future of intense familial rivalry. (This theme of barrenness, a prelude to divine intervention, will recur with three more significant women in the scriptures.) In contrast, Leah, though unloved, is immediately fertile. Before the chapter ends, she bears Jacob his first four sons: Reuben, Simeon, Levi, and Judah. These boys are not merely children; they are the founding patriarchs of the first four of the twelve tribes of Israel, anchoring the future nation in a story of love, deception, and ultimately, God's overarching providence.

*****

The thirtieth chapter of Genesis unfolds as a tense domestic drama, set against the harsh realities of ancient Near Eastern life and the intense rivalry between two sisters, Rachel and Leah. The chapter opens with Rachel, Jacob's beloved but barren wife, engulfed by a bitter envy. Her sister, Leah—the wife Jacob was tricked into marrying—had now borne him four sons in succession: Reuben, Simeon, Levi, and Judah. Each birth was a public celebration that served as a private agony for Rachel, a stark reminder of her own unfulfilled womb and a perceived failure in her primary societal role.

This deep-seated anguish finally overflowed into a desperate and dramatic ultimatum directed at her husband. "Give me children," she demanded, her voice laced with the pain of years of disappointment, "or else I will die!" Her words were less a request and more a declaration of a life not worth living. Jacob, aroused to anger by the unfairness of the accusation—for he well knew the source of life was divine—retorted sharply, "Am I in the place of God, who has withheld from you the fruit of the womb?" His response highlights the ancient understanding that procreation was ultimately a blessing bestowed by the divine.

Refusing to remain passive, Rachel invoked a well-established custom of the time. She presented her maid, Bilhah, to Jacob, saying, "Here is my maid Bilhah; go in to her, that she may bear upon my knees, and that I too may have children through her." The phrase "bear upon my knees" was a specific legal and symbolic act. Upon birth, the child would be immediately placed on the knees of the barren wife, formalizing her legal adoption of the child as her own, making it her legitimate heir. Through this custom, Bilhah became a matriarch of Israel, giving birth to Jacob's fifth son, Dan (meaning "He has judged"), and his sixth son, Naphtali (meaning "My wrestling").

This strategic move did not go unnoticed by Leah. Having believed her own season of childbearing was over, she saw Rachel's success through a surrogate and decided to employ the same tactic. Not to be outdone, she gave her own maid, Zilpah, to Jacob. Zilpah, too, earned her status as a matriarch, bearing Jacob's seventh son, Gad (meaning "Good fortune" or "A troop"), and his eighth son, Asher (meaning "Happy am I!").

The rivalry then took a surprising turn during the wheat harvest. Leah's eldest son, Reuben, discovered mandrakes in the field. These yellow, aromatic fruits (from the Mandragora officinarum plant) were highly prized in the ancient world for their purported aphrodisiac and fertility-enhancing properties, deeply embedded in the folklore of the region.

When Rachel learned of the discovery, she approached her sister with a plea: "Please give me some of your son's mandrakes." Leah, whose resentment had festered for years, seized the moment. Her retort was a raw outburst of pent-up frustration: "Is it a small matter that you have taken away my husband? Would you take away my son's mandrakes also?" This pointed reference to Jacob's clear romantic preference for Rachel cut to the heart of their lifelong competition.

In a moment of desperate negotiation, Rachel offered a startling trade: "Therefore, Jacob will lie with you tonight in exchange for your son's mandrakes." The exchange reduces the sacredness of the marital act to a bartered commodity, highlighting the depths of Rachel's obsession and Leah's longing for connection. Leah agreed, and that evening she waylaid Jacob, announcing, "You must come in to me, for I have hired you with my son's mandrakes."

Ironically, it was not the mandrakes but this very encounter that proved fruitful for Leah. God "listened to Leah," and she conceived once more, bearing Jacob his ninth and tenth sons: Issachar (meaning "There is reward") and Zebulun (meaning "Dwelling"). She also later bore his only named daughter, Dinah.

Finally, after years of anguish, prayer, and rivalry, "God remembered Rachel." He heeded her prayers and opened her womb. She conceived and gave birth to a son, declaring,

"God has taken away my reproach." She named him Joseph (meaning "May he add"), praying, "May the LORD add to me another son!" This child, Jacob's eleventh son, immediately became his most cherished and favorite, a preference that would later fuel immense family conflict.

The chapter closes by shifting focus from the domestic sphere to Jacob's professional life. Having fulfilled his fourteen years of service for Laban to marry his daughters, Jacob was now ready to provide for his own large household and return to his homeland. Laban, however, keenly aware that the blessings of prosperity upon his own estate were directly linked to Jacob's presence (as he admits, "I have learned by divination that the LORD has blessed me because of you"), begged him to stay. They struck a new wage agreement, whereby Jacob would take all the speckled, spotted, and black sheep and goats from the flock as his payment. Through a combination of shrewd animal husbandry—using peeled rods of poplar, almond, and plane trees at the watering troughs to influence the strength and patterning of the offspring—and divine blessing, Jacob prospered exceedingly. He grew his flock to be vast and strong, while Laban's became comparatively weak, setting the stage for their eventual and inevitable parting.

*****

In the escalating tension of Genesis 31, we learn that Jacob, who has prospered greatly under God's blessing, overhears the bitter and resentful murmurs of Laban's sons. They accuse him of stripping their father's wealth to build his own, claiming, "Jacob has taken all that was our father's, and from what was our father's he has gained all this wealth." Jacob also observes a palpable shift in Laban's own demeanor toward him; the once warm, if manipulative, relationship has cooled into suspicion and hostility.

Recognizing that his time in Haran has reached its end, Jacob does not act alone. He summons his two wives, Rachel and Leah, to the fields where his flocks are kept, creating a private space away from the household. There, he articulates his case for departure. He meticulously recounts the full history of his twenty years of service: how their father, Laban, has consistently changed his wages and dealt deceitfully with him. Most importantly, Jacob frames his entire narrative not as a story of his own cunning, but as a testimony of divine intervention. He tells them how the God of his father, Isaac, has been with him, how in a dream the Angel of God revealed that the streaked and spotted lambs were a divine gift, and how God has ultimately taken their father's livestock and given it to Jacob as rightful wages. This appeal is crucial—he is asking them to choose between their natal family and their husband's divinely-ordained journey.

The sisters, who have their own grievances, wholeheartedly agree with Jacob's assessment. They feel utterly alienated from their father, lamenting, "Is there any portion or inheritance left to us in our father's house? Are we not regarded by him as foreigners? For he has sold us, and he has been devouring our money." They see no future for themselves or their children in Laban's household and fully align themselves with Jacob's destiny, declaring, "Now then, whatever God has said to you, do." The decision is made to depart for Canaan, the land of Jacob's father, Isaac.

The escape, however, is fraught with peril from the start. Unbeknownst to Jacob, his beloved wife Rachel has committed a grave and dangerous act. As they flee, she secretly steals her father's household gods, the teraphim. These idols were not merely religious objects; they were likely linked to inheritance rights and clan leadership, making their theft a serious crime. This single act of deception sets the stage for a dramatic confrontation.

Three days into the journey, Laban discovers their flight. Enraged, he gathers his kinsmen and pursues Jacob with a small army, finally catching up to him after seven days in the hill country of Gilead. On the eve of what Laban surely intended as a violent recrimination, God intervenes directly. In a dream, the God of Jacob's fathers speaks to Laban, issuing a stern warning: "Be careful not to say anything to Jacob, either good or bad." This divine injunction forces Laban to temper his rage, though his accusation remains sharp.

When he confronts Jacob, his primary charge is not the clandestine flight—which Jacob justifies by his fear of having his wives taken from him—but the theft of his gods. Furious and humiliated, Laban cries, "What have you done, that you have tricked me and driven away my daughters like captives of the sword?... Why did you steal my gods?"

Blind to Rachel's guilt and righteous in his indignation, Jacob makes a fatalistic declaration: "Anyone with whom you find your gods shall not live." He grants Laban unrestricted permission to search the entire camp, unknowingly condemning his own wife. Laban meticulously combs through every tent, from Jacob's to Leah's to the two maidservants', finding nothing. Finally, he enters Rachel's tent.

Rachel, however, had cleverly hidden the idols inside her camel's saddlebag and was sitting on them. As her father rummaged through her belongings, she remained seated, offering a deft and culturally untouchable excuse: "Let not my lord be angry that I cannot rise before you, for the way of women is upon me." By citing her menstrual period, she invoked a state of ritual impurity that would discourage any further search or physical contact. Laban, deceived by his own daughter, left her tent empty-handed and humiliated.

This pivotal moment of near-disaster forces a settlement. With his accusation proven false and his authority checked by God, a humbled Laban is forced to reconcile. It is in this context of exhausted conflict that Jacob delivers a powerful soliloquy, recounting the immense hardships of his twenty years of service—the scorching heat, the freezing cold, the sleepless nights, and Laban's constant deception. He emphasizes that his survival and prosperity were solely due to the faithfulness of "the God of my father, the God of Abraham and the Fear of Isaac."

The chapter concludes not with further strife, but with a covenant. Jacob and Laban erect a stone pillar and a heap of stones as a witness and a boundary marker between them. They share a ceremonial meal and swear an oath before God that neither will cross this boundary with hostile intent. Laban blesses his daughters and grandchildren and returns to his home, while Jacob continues his journey toward the promised land, finally free from his father-in-law's grasp, yet now carrying within his own household the secret of Rachel's deceit.

*****

Our narrative resumes in the turbulent thirty-fourth chapter of Genesis, finding the patriarch Jacob and his burgeoning family no longer as wandering nomads but tentatively settled in the land of Canaan. They had encamped on a parcel of land purchased near the Hivite city of Shechem from Hamor, the city's prince. This purchase represented a significant, and perhaps perilous, step: for the first time, the family of the promise—the heirs of Abraham and Isaac—were putting down roots outside their kinship group, dwelling as aliens and sojourners amidst a powerful and established Canaanite community.

It is in this tense atmosphere of fragile coexistence that the devastating "Dinah Incident" unfolds. Dinah, the daughter of Jacob by Leah, ventured out to visit the women of the land—a simple act of youthful curiosity and a desire for connection. However, her outing ended in tragedy. Shechem, the son of Prince Hamor, saw her, seized her, and lay with her by force, violating her profoundly. The biblical text offers a complex and disturbing portrait of her assailant, noting that following this heinous act, "his soul was drawn to Dinah... he loved the young woman and spoke tenderly to her." This psychological detail does not excuse the violation but rather deepens the tragedy, painting a picture of a spoiled prince used to taking what he wanted, who then, in a twisted turn, believed his genuine affection could erase his initial brutal crime.

The news reached Jacob's sons in the fields, and their reaction was one of white-hot, righteous fury. They returned home stunned and smoldering with indignation. The violation of their sister was an unspeakable offense, a stain on their family's honor that demanded a severe response. Their rage was then compounded by an astonishing proposal from Shechem and his father, Hamor. Arriving at Jacob's camp, the prince and his father argued not for justice or atonement, but for merger. Shechem, smitten, wished to marry Dinah. Hamor, seeing a political and economic opportunity, expanded the offer: intermarriage between their peoples, open trade, and the chance for Jacob's clan to own land freely among them. To the brothers, this was not a peace offering but the ultimate insult—an attempt to casually purchase their sister and assimilate their unique family into Canaanite culture after such a grievous wrong.

It was in this caldron of fury and insult that a cunning and brutal plan of revenge was conceived. Speaking with deceptive civility, Jacob's sons, led by the second and third eldest, Simeon and Levi, gave their answer. They declared it impossible to give their sister to an uncircumcised man, for that would be a disgrace. Yet, they offered a sinister loophole: if every male in Shechem's city would undergo the sacred covenant of circumcision—the very sign of God's promise to Abraham—then they would consent to the marriage and the proposed integration.

To Shechem and Hamor, the price seemed not only agreeable but advantageous. They saw a ritual, not a ruse; a religious formality that would unlock great wealth and a desirable bride for the prince. They failed to comprehend the deep spiritual significance of the act to Israel or the murderous deception in the brothers' hearts. Persuading the men of their city with promises of Jacob's future wealth and livestock, Hamor and Shechem ensured that every able-bodied male underwent the procedure.

The stage was now set for the horrific climax. On the third day, when the pain from the operation was at its most excruciating and the men were feverish and utterly incapacitated, Simeon and Levi, Dinah's full brothers, sprang their trap. Armed with swords and fueled by a volatile mix of vengeance and zeal, they descended upon the defenseless city. They showed no mercy, slaughtering Prince Hamor, his son Shechem, and every newly circumcised male. In a orgy of violence, they turned a rite of covenant into an instrument of massacre.

The other sons of Jacob then arrived to partake in the plunder. They looted the city, seized its wealth and livestock, and took the women and children captive, compounding one sin with another—theft and enslavement. What began as an act of retribution for their sister had devolved into a wholesale atrocity that dishonored the very God whose covenant sign they had profaned.

The chapter closes not with victory, but with a profound and somber tension. Jacob, the father, confronted his sons. His wrath was not directed at the initial crime against Dinah, but at the catastrophic political consequences of their actions. "You have brought trouble on me," he lamented, "by making me odious to the inhabitants of the land... and since I am few in number, they will gather themselves against me and attack me; I shall be destroyed, both I and my household." He saw his hard-won peace and security evaporating, replaced by the terrifying prospect of annihilation from vengeful neighboring tribes. Simeon and Levi's retort was swift and unrepentant: "Should he treat our sister like a prostitute?" Their question hangs in the air, unresolved—a stark illustration of the violent clash between human passion and divine purpose, a moment where justice was demanded but righteousness was utterly abandoned.

*****

From that pivotal and traumatic moment in Shechem, the figure of Dinah recedes entirely from the biblical narrative, her voice and fate remaining an enduring mystery. The text shifts its focus decisively back to the patriarchal line, detailing the next critical phase in the formation of the nation of Israel.

The action resumes in Chapter 35 with a divine imperative: God commands Jacob to lead his household to Bethel, the very place where decades earlier he had vowed to God after his vision of a ladder reaching to heaven. Recognizing the profound spiritual significance of this journey, Jacob understands that his family, recently tainted by the violence and idolatry of Shechem, must be purified. He therefore issues a sweeping command for his entire household to rid themselves of the foreign gods they had accumulated—perhaps the teraphim Rachel had stolen from Laban or idols taken as plunder from Shechem. Furthermore, he instructs them to ritually cleanse themselves and change their garments, symbolizing a shedding of their old, polluted identities and preparing to approach the holy place in a state of ceremonial purity.

Upon their arrival at Bethel, Jacob builds an altar, and God once again appears to him in a powerful theophany. This encounter is profoundly life-changing, serving as a divine reaffirmation of the covenant. In a moment echoing the experience of his grandfather Abraham, Jacob receives a new name: Israel, which means "he struggles with God." This name is a perpetual reminder of his mysterious and wrestling encounter with the divine being at Peniel, where he persevered and demanded a blessing. God then elaborates on the covenant promises, declaring, "I am God Almighty [El Shaddai]. Be fruitful and multiply; a nation and a company of nations shall proceed from you, and kings shall come from your body. The land which I gave Abraham and Isaac I give to you; and to your descendants after you I give this land." This powerful proclamation not only reaffirms Jacob's destiny but also solidifies his role as a direct inheritor of the promises made to his forefathers.

Fortified by this covenant renewal, the newly named Israel and his large family depart Bethel. As they journey toward Ephrath (later known as Bethlehem), a profound tragedy strikes. Rachel, Jacob's beloved wife, goes into labor. The delivery is agonizingly difficult, and despite the efforts of the midwife, it becomes clear she will not survive. With her final breaths, she gives birth to Israel's twelfth and final son. In her despair and pain, she names him Ben-Oni, meaning "son of my sorrow." Heartbroken yet perhaps seeking to preserve a legacy of hope from the moment of profound loss, Jacob renames the infant Benjamin, "son of the right hand" or "son of my happiness," a name signifying strength, favor, and a blessed future. Rachel was buried there on the road to Ephrath, and Jacob, in an enduring gesture of grief and love, erected a pillar upon her grave—a monument that would be known for generations as the Pillar of Rachel's Tomb.

The chapter concludes by formally listing the twelve sons born to Jacob, the future patriarchs of the twelve tribes of Israel, cementing the complete structure of the chosen nation. Finally, the narrative notes the death of Isaac at the ripe old age of 180. In a show of reconciliation and familial duty, his two sons, Israel (Jacob) and Esau, come together to bury him alongside his wife Rebekah in the cave of Machpelah, the family tomb where his parents, Abraham and Sarah, also lay at rest. This act brings a measure of closure to a generation, fully passing the covenant mantle to Jacob and his twelve sons.

Leah's death is left out of scripture, a silent contrast to the dramatic passing of her sister-wife. While Rachel's grave is marked alone on a roadside, what we do know is that Leah is buried in the family tomb in Machpelah, a quiet honor granted to the less-loved but ultimately faithful wife who bore the majority of the tribal founders and secured her place in the heart of the covenant's legacy.

The Courageous Matriarch: Tamar

Before concluding the book of Genesis, it is crucial to pause and examine the pivotal, albeit unsettling, story contained in chapter 38. This narrative provides a stark portrait of ancient Near Eastern customs and introduces one of the Bible's most courageous and unexpected heroines: Tamar.

Tamar's story begins with her marriage into the family of Judah, one of Jacob's twelve sons. She was given as a wife to Judah's firstborn son, Er. However, Er was described as profoundly "wicked in the sight of the Lord," and as divine retribution for his actions, the Lord struck him down, leaving Tamar a childless widow.

Following the custom of levirate marriage—a practice designed to provide for widows and continue a deceased man's lineage—Judah instructed his second son, Onan, to marry Tamar and produce an heir for his late brother. Onan, however, harbored selfish motives. He understood that any son born from this union would be considered Er's legal heir and would inherit Er's portion of the family estate, thereby diminishing Onan's own future inheritance. In a calculated act of defiance, Onan "spilled his seed on the ground" whenever he was with Tamar, ensuring she would not conceive. This act of deliberate disobedience and his failure to fulfill his familial duty "displeased the Lord greatly," and consequently, Onan was also put to death.

Now twice-widowed and still without the security of a son, Tamar was promised to Judah's youngest and only remaining son, Shelah. Judah, perhaps superstitiously fearing for Shelah's life, told Tamar to return to her father's house as a widow "until my son Shelah grows up." In reality, Judah had no intention of honoring this promise, leaving Tamar in a state of social and economic limbo for years.

The plot advanced when Judah's own wife died. After his period of mourning, he journeyed with his friend Hirah the Adullamite to Timnah to oversee the shearing of his sheep, a time of celebration and festivity. Tamar, learning of his travel plans and realizing that Shelah was now a grown man yet had not been given to her, took a daring and desperate gamble. Disguising herself with a veil to look like a cult prostitute (a qedeshah), she positioned herself conspicuously at the entrance to Enaim, a town on the road to Timnah.

As she had anticipated, Judah saw her and, not recognizing his daughter-in-law, propositioned her. They negotiated a price: a young goat from his flock. As a guarantee for this future payment, Tamar shrewdly asked for a pledge. Judah gave her his personal signet ring (used for sealing documents), the cord from which it hung, and his distinctive shepherd's staff—items that served as unmistakable identifiers of his identity. From this encounter, Tamar conceived.

Afterward, Tamar returned home, resuming her life as a widow, while Judah attempted to send the promised goat with his friend Hirah to retrieve his pledges. The "prostitute," of course, was nowhere to be found, and the men of the area denied any knowledge of her, leaving Judah unable to reclaim his items.

About three months later, Judah received shocking news: his daughter-in-law Tamar was pregnant, apparently as a result of "harlotry." Outraged by what he perceived as a violation of his family's honor and oblivious to his own role, Judah pronounced a harsh sentence: "Bring her out and let her be burned!"

As Tamar was being brought forth for execution, she sent a message to her father-in-law along with his personal items, stating, "I am with child by the man to whom these things belong. Please determine whose these are." Confronted with the undeniable evidence of his own signet, cord, and staff, Judah was forced into a moment of profound self-awareness and public humility. He immediately recognized that his own failure to provide Shelah had driven her to this extreme act and that he, the righteous judge, was the guilty party. He declared, "She is more righteous than I, since I did not give her to my son Shelah." This confession absolved Tamar completely.

The chapter concludes with the account of Tamar's delivery, which was as dramatic as the events that led to it. She was pregnant with twins. During the difficult birth, one infant (Zerah) extended his hand, and the midwife tied a scarlet thread around it to mark him as the firstborn. However, he drew his hand back, and his brother (Perez) unexpectedly pushed through and was born first. The midwife exclaimed, "Why did you break through for yourself? This breach be upon you!" Thus, the firstborn was named Perez, meaning "breach" or "breakthrough," and his brother was named Zerah, meaning "brightness" or "dawn."

This story, while seemingly a digression in the Joseph narrative, is of tremendous theological importance. Tamar's courageous fight for her rights and survival within a patriarchal system secured the lineage of Judah. Her son, Perez, is explicitly listed as a direct ancestor of King David (Ruth 4:18-22) and, through him, of Jesus Christ (Matthew 1:3). Thus, Tamar is honored as a vital link in the messianic line, a testament to how God often works through the most unexpected and marginalized figures to fulfill His promises.

*****

As we turn the final page on the Book of Genesis, a foundational text rich with patriarchs and promises, it is crucial to pause and reflect on the often understated yet profoundly impactful roles of the women in its closing chapters (39-50). Their stories are a complex tapestry of human nature—featuring virtue and vice, silence and voice, tragedy and triumph. It is important to note that not all women listed here are presented as moral exemplars; rather, they are pivotal agents whose actions, whether righteous or deceitful, became inextricably woven into the grand, divine scheme of Israel's founding narrative. Their presence moves the plot forward with undeniable force, setting the stage for the epic story of Exodus to come.

Potiphar's Wife (Genesis 39): An Agent of Providence Through Betrayal The first woman we encounter is the unnamed wife of Potiphar, Pharaoh's captain of the guard. Her story is one of potent desire and devastating falsehood. Joseph, a handsome and trustworthy young Hebrew slave, had found favor in Potiphar's house and was put in charge of all his affairs. However, Potiphar's wife "cast her eyes upon Joseph" and repeatedly propositioned him, saying, "Lie with me."

Joseph's refusal was not merely based on loyalty to his master but on a profound theological conviction. He declared, "...How then can I do this great wickedness, and sin against God?" This establishes a key theme: Joseph's identity and integrity are rooted in his relationship with God, even in a foreign land. His virtue, however, incites her humiliation and rage. On one fateful day, as she cornered him and he fled her grasp, she seized his outer garment, tearing it from his body.

Holding this tangible "evidence," she expertly inverted the narrative. She called her household guards and, upon her husband's return, crafted a damning story. She used the garment as proof, accusing Joseph not of rejecting her, but of attempting to violate her. She strategically framed her cries of alarm as a defense of her honor, asking, "See, [Potiphar] has brought among us a Hebrew to insult us!" Her accusation played on ethnic prejudices and fears, ensuring Joseph's condemnation. In his anger—likely as much about the public dishonor as the alleged crime—Potiphar had Joseph imprisoned in the royal dungeon.

Why was this shameful, traumatic event so critical? Humanly speaking, it was a profound injustice. Yet, divinely, it was the essential catalyst for everything that followed. The prison was where Joseph would meet Pharaoh's chief cupbearer and baker, interpret their dreams, and eventually be recommended to a troubled Pharaoh years later. This unjust imprisonment, triggered by a woman's lie, was the necessary conduit for Joseph to ascend to the position of vizier of Egypt. There, he would interpret Pharaoh's dreams, oversee the storing of grain, and ultimately save the known world from a seven-year famine. This act of salvation would also directly lead to the preservation of his own family—the family of Israel—and set the stage for their eventual descent into Egypt. Furthermore, it was this high office that granted Joseph the status to marry the next woman on our list.

Asenath (Genesis 41:45, 50): The Mother of Tribes Asenath enters the narrative as a symbol of Joseph's complete integration and exalted status in Egyptian society. Following his interpretation of Pharaoh's dreams and his appointment as second-in-command over all Egypt, Pharaoh bestows upon him a new Egyptian name, Zaphenath-paneah, and gives him "Asenath, the daughter of Poti-phera, priest of On, as his wife." This was a politically astute move, aligning Joseph with the powerful priestly class of Heliopolis (On). Unlike the fraught relationship with Potiphar's wife, his union with Asenath is presented as legitimate, blessed, and fruitful.

Before the years of famine began, Asenath bore Joseph two sons. In naming them, Joseph explicitly acknowledged God's hand in his remarkable journey from suffering to glory. He named the firstborn Manasseh, meaning "Making to forget," for he said, "God has made me forget all my hardship and all my father's house." The second he named Ephraim, meaning "Fruitfulness," declaring, "God has made me fruitful in the land of my affliction."

Though Asenath herself has no recorded dialogue, her role is monumentally important. She is the mother of the two half-Egyptian sons whom the aging, blind Jacob will later intentionally and prophetically bless (Genesis 48). In a stunning twist, Jacob elevates the younger Ephraim over the firstborn Manasseh, ensuring that both boys are adopted into the direct line of Israel's inheritance. Their names would forever be borne by two of the most powerful tribes of the Northern Kingdom of Israel. Thus, through Asenath, the line of Joseph is secured and becomes central to the future identity of the nation.

With the stories of these women—one whose malice propelled a nation toward destiny, and another whose motherhood helped form it—we close the book on Genesis. Their legacies, along with those of the matriarchs before them, are carried into the land of Egypt with Jacob's family. Our next stop on this journey is Exodus, where the seeds planted in Genesis will sprout into a nation longing for liberation, and where new, formidable female figures will arise to defy a Pharaoh and shape the destiny of their people.

The Courageous Midwives: Shiphrah and Puah

Our journey takes us to the foundational and dramatic book of Exodus, a narrative that forms the bedrock of Israel's identity as a nation liberated by God. While traditional study often focuses on the spectacular miracles of the plagues, the parting of the Red Sea, and the towering figures of Moses and Aaron, today we shift our lens. We will move these well-known stories to the background, bringing into sharp focus the often-overlooked but pivotal women whose courage and defiance set the entire story of redemption in motion.

Roughly four centuries have passed since the death of Joseph, the Hebrew vizier who saved Egypt from famine. In that time, the gratitude of the Egyptian court has faded into distant memory. A new dynasty of Pharaohs has risen, leaders who "did not know Joseph," meaning they felt no historical debt to his people. This Pharaoh viewed the Israelites not as honored guests but as a formidable internal threat. Their prolific growth and cohesion as a people fueled a paranoia that they might side with Egypt's enemies in a conflict. This fear catalyzed a brutal policy of oppression: the Israelites were enslaved and subjected to a regime of backbreaking labor, tasked with building the store cities of Pithom and Rameses under the crushing weight of bricks and mortar.

Yet, in a powerful act of divine irony, the harder the Egyptians oppressed them, the more "the Israelites multiplied and spread." Pharaoh's strategy of attrition had failed utterly. It is at this critical juncture that we meet the first two heroines of Exodus: Shiphrah and Puah. These women were the chief Hebrew midwives, entrusted with the sacred duty of ushering new life into the world. The text highlights a crucial detail about their character: they were "righteous women who feared God." This was not a simple religious preference; it was the core of their identity and the source of their moral compass, which would soon be tested by the highest power in the land.

Pharaoh, desperate to curb the Hebrew population, summoned Shiphrah and Puah and issued a monstrous, genocidal command: when they attended a Hebrew birth, they were to kill any newborn boy but allow the girls to live. This covert, clinical order was designed to slowly eliminate the military threat of future Hebrew men while allowing the assimilation of women into Egyptian society.

Faced with an unimaginable moral dilemma—to obey the sovereign of the most powerful empire on earth or to obey their conscience and their God—Shiphrah and Puah made a conscious choice. Their fear of a holy and just God far outweighed their fear of a wrathful Pharaoh. They quietly subverted the decree, allowing every child, boy and girl, to live. When Pharaoh eventually discovered that Hebrew boys were still thriving, he summoned the midwives for a terrifying accountability meeting.

Their response to his interrogation was a masterstroke of cunning and wisdom. They said, "Because the Hebrew women are not like the Egyptian women; for they are lively and give birth before the midwives come to them." This brilliant answer accomplished several things: it flattered Egyptian cultural assumptions about robust "foreign" women, it provided a perfectly plausible excuse that Pharaoh could not disprove, and, most importantly, it protected the lives of the mothers and their children. They used Pharaoh's own prejudice to outwit him.

The narrative tells us that "God was good to the midwives." This favor was manifested tangibly: He "provided families for them," a profound blessing for women whose profession brought life to others. Furthermore, the Israelite people continued to grow mightily. The courageous defiance of two women had thwarted the first official attempt at their destruction.

Sadly, this setback did not deter Pharaoh. Enraged and more determined, he bypassed the midwives entirely and issued a public and horrifying decree to all his people: "Every Hebrew boy that is born you must throw into the Nile, but let every girl live." This escalated the secretive command into an open, state-sanctioned pogrom. It was this brutal edict, a direct result of the midwives' failed mission, that set the stage for the next act of feminine courage and set in motion the events that would lead to the introduction of Israel's great deliverer, lawgiver, and first true Rabbi: Moses. His story, too, would begin not on a battlefield or in a palace, but through the defiant actions of more women—his mother, his sister, and an Egyptian princess.

Jochebed and the princess

The second chapter of Exodus opens with a poignant union in the midst of oppression: a man from the house of Levi took a Levite woman as his wife. Though they are not named in this passage, later scripture (Numbers 26:59) reveals their identities as Amram and Jochebed, anchoring this family within the priestly lineage of Israel.

Their story leaps forward with the birth of a son, a child described as being "fine" or beautiful. For Jochebed, this blessing was also a source of immense terror, as Pharaoh's genocidal decree hung over every Hebrew male infant. Driven by a mother's fierce love and ingenuity, she managed to conceal the child for three months. However, as he grew stronger and his cries louder, hiding him within their humble dwelling became an impossible risk.

Faced with no other choice, Jochebed conceived a brilliant and daring plan. Drawing on her lifelong experience as a resident of the Nile Delta, she crafted a small, waterproofed ark or basket from papyrus reeds (bulrushes), carefully sealing its seams with tar and pitch to make it watertight. She then laid her precious son inside, upon a soft bed of reeds, and placed the basket among the vegetation at the edge of the great river.

This was not an act of desperate abandonment, but a meticulously calculated strategy. Jochebed, a slave who had lived her entire life near the Nile, was intimately familiar with the rhythms of Egyptian royalty. She knew the habits of the Pharaoh's daughter, whom Jewish tradition names Bithyah (or Batyah). Historical context informs us that ritual purity was paramount to the Egyptians, and royalty would bathe in the sacred waters of the Nile multiple times a day. Jochebed would not have placed the infant in a sealed basket during the scorching heat of the afternoon; this act was deliberately timed for the princess's likely morning ablutions, when the waters were cooler and the princess's entourage would be present.

Jochebed's foresight was profound. She knew the princess would come to that general area, and she banked on a critical truth: that a woman's heart, especially that of a royal daughter, would show compassion toward a helpless infant before any male official would. To oversee the plan, she stationed the baby's older sister, Miriam (as named later in Exodus 15:20), at a discreet distance to witness the event and intervene at the precise moment.

As anticipated, Princess Bithyah arrived at the river with her attendants and handmaidens for her bath. Her eye caught the unusual basket nestled in the reeds, and she sent one of her maids to retrieve it. Upon opening it, she discovered the crying Hebrew boy. Despite him being one of the children of the enslaved people her father sought to eliminate, her heart was stirred with immediate pity and compassion. She may not have known the God of Israel, YHWH, but she possessed an innate righteousness and kindness. She likely recognized his Hebrew origin by the sign of his circumcision, yet this did not harden her heart against him.

Seeing the princess's compassion, Miriam seized her divinely appointed moment. She stepped forward and, with remarkable poise for a young girl, offered to find a Hebrew wet-nurse from among the women to care for the baby. Princess Bithyah agreed, and Miriam rushed to fetch none other than the child's own mother, Jochebed. In a stunning twist of providential irony, the princess commissioned the baby's mother to nurse him, even offering to pay her wages to raise her own son. Jochebed's faith and clever plan were thus overwhelmingly rewarded.

After the child was weaned, he was brought back to the palace. Princess Bithyah formally adopted him as her own son and named him Moses (Moshe), declaring, "I drew him out of the water." With this, the narrative of his miraculous infancy closes. Jochebed, though later mentioned in genealogical records, recedes from the active story, her ultimate fate remaining unknown.

The scene then shifts abruptly, spanning decades into the future. Now a grown man, Moses, aware of his Hebrew heritage, witnessed the brutal oppression of his people. One day, upon seeing an Egyptian taskmaster beating a Hebrew slave, his anger erupted, and he killed the Egyptian. When Pharaoh learned of this act of treason, Moses was forced to flee for his life into the wilderness of Midian. There, exhausted at a well, he encountered the seven daughters of the priest of Midian, Reuel (also known as Jethro), setting the stage for the next woman of the Word.

The Priest's Daughter: Zipporah

Following his narrow escape from the wrath of Pharaoh, Moses sought refuge in the distant, arid wilderness of Midian. It is here, sitting in the quiet isolation of exile, that our narrative resumes. Moses rests by a local well, unaware that he is about to intervene in a scene of long-standing social prejudice.

The daughters of Reuel (also known as Jethro), the local priest, arrived at the well to water their father's flock. They were quickly confronted by a group of male shepherds who, fueled by the chauvinistic belief that guarding the water supply was exclusively a man's domain, forcefully drove the women away. Seeing this injustice, Moses—embodying the protective spirit that once led him to strike down the Egyptian taskmaster—rose to defend the sisters, utilizing his strength to help them draw water for their livestock.

The sisters returned home uncharacteristically early, startling their father. When they recounted how an "Egyptian" stranger had defended them and watered their flocks, Jethro immediately sought to honor this act of chivalry. He questioned why they had left the man behind and instructed them to bring him to their home. While the text refers to Moses as an "Egyptian"—likely due to his attire, speech, and etiquette—Reuel, as a man of great discernment, would have undoubtedly recognized the Hebrew identity of the man who married his daughter, Zipporah.

Zipporah, a shepherdess of distinct resolve, became Moses' wife, and in time, she bore him a son named Gershom, marking the beginning of Moses' new life in the desert.
This period of Moses' life often invites scholarly debate regarding Zipporah's heritage. Some point to Numbers 12:1, where Miriam and Aaron criticize Moses for marrying a "Cushite" (often translated as Ethiopian) woman. However, it is vital to contextualize this: this dispute occurred forty years after his marriage to Zipporah. Furthermore, geography dictates the distinction; Moses fled to Midian, located in the northwest of the Arabian Peninsula, while Cush (Ethiopia) lay far to the south of Egypt. Jewish tradition largely suggests that Moses may have taken a second wife in later years, distinct from Zipporah. Regarding Zipporah herself, the Midianites were descendants of Abraham and his wife Keturah—specifically through their son, Midian—establishing that she was of Semitic, Hebrew-adjacent lineage, not Cushite.

As the narrative progresses toward the burning bush and the call to return to Egypt, we learn of the birth of a second son, Eliezer. Soon, Moses, Zipporah, and their boys set out for Egypt. Yet, the journey was interrupted by a harrowing, enigmatic encounter. Exodus 4:24 records that at a nighttime encampment, the Lord sought to kill someone—likely one of the sons who remained uncircumcised. In a moment of urgent, decisive action, Zipporah performed the rite of circumcision herself, touching the foreskin to Moses' feet as an act of atonement. Following this incident, Zipporah returned to her father's household, separating from Moses while he faced the monumental plagues of Egypt. She remained in Midian, missing the climactic liberation and the parting of the Red Sea. It was not until the Israelites reached Mount Sinai that Jethro escorted her and the boys back to Moses. After this reunion, Zipporah's presence in the biblical account quietly recedes. History leaves us in silence as to whether she ultimately entered the Promised Land, her legacy remaining anchored in that singular act of devotion at the desert encampment.

The liberator's sister: Miriam

While we previously touched upon Miriam's role within the narrative of "Jochebed and the Princess," her significance in the tapestry of Israel's history deserves a much more comprehensive exploration. Miriam was far more than a supporting character; she was a strategist, a leader, and a spiritual cornerstone for her people.

As the eldest child of Jochebed and Amram, Miriam's story begins with an act of profound courage and precocious wisdom. While her infant brother Moses floated in a reed basket upon the Nile, it was Miriam who stood at a distance, vigilantly keeping watch. When Pharaoh's daughter discovered the child, Miriam did not flee in fear. Instead, she stepped forward with a bold diplomatic proposal, ultimately securing their own mother, Jochebed, to serve as Moses' wet nurse. This clever intervention ensured that Moses was not only kept safe but was raised with an understanding of his Hebrew heritage.

Following the dramatic exodus from Egypt, we see Miriam emerge not just as a sister, but as a public leader. The next major milestone occurs in Exodus chapter 15, immediately following the miraculous crossing of the Red Sea. After the Egyptian army was defeated, the air was filled with the sound of triumph. Scripture records two distinct responses: the "Song of Moses," an epic, lengthy martial hymn detailing God's victory in battle, and the "Song of Miriam."

In this moment, Miriam is officially recognized as the first woman in Scripture to bear the title of Prophetess. Leading a procession of women, she took up her tambourine—an instrument preserved even through the haste of the flight from Egypt—and led the assembly in rhythmic praise and dance. Her song was short, punchy, and potent, a call-and-response that galvanized the spirits of the liberated slaves. She functioned as a worship leader for half the nation, cementing her status as a vital spiritual authority alongside her brothers.

The narrative then shifts to a more complex and somber chapter in Numbers 12. While the conflict began as a critique of Moses' marriage to a Cushite woman (a topic explored in our study of Zipporah), the underlying issue was a challenge of spiritual authority. Miriam and Aaron questioned why Moses held a singular status, asking, "Has the Lord indeed spoken only through Moses? Has He not spoken through us also?"

The response from the Heavens was immediate and terrifying. The Lord descended in a pillar of cloud, standing at the door of the Tabernacle and summoning the three siblings. God's rebuke was a definitive declaration of Moses' unique position. He explained that while He speaks to other prophets through visions and enigmatic dreams, He speaks to Moses "mouth to mouth"—plainly and face-to-face. God's question, "Why then were you not afraid to speak against My servant Moses?" echoed with divine weight.

As the cloud lifted, the physical manifestation of God's displeasure became visible: Miriam was struck with leprosy, her skin turning as white as snow. This was a devastating blow, both physically and socially. Aaron, seeing his sister's condition, was moved to immediate repentance, and Moses, in a beautiful display of brotherly love, cried out to God for her healing.

God, in His mercy, answered the prayer but insisted on a period of ritual purification. Miriam was commanded to stay outside the camp for seven days. This week must have been a season of deep isolation and harrowing reflection for the prophetess. However, the Bible notes a touching detail: the entire nation of Israel refused to march on; they waited in place for those seven days until Miriam was brought back into the fold. This gesture showed the immense respect and love the people held for her.

Miriam's journey continued through the wilderness for decades. She remained a pillar of the community until her death, thirty-eight years after the incident of leprosy. At the age of 126, while the Israelites were stationed at Kadesh, Miriam passed away and was buried there.

Ultimately, Miriam belongs to that transitionary generation of leaders who saw the wonders of Egypt and the hardships of the desert but were destined to fall short of the physical Promised Land. Along with Aaron and Moses, she died before the crossing of the Jordan. Yet, her legacy as a protector of her family and a prophetic voice for her nation remains an enduring testament to the power of a woman's leadership in the biblical epic.

*****

Before we transition to the book of Joshua to meet our next courageous woman of the Word, I feel a significant and honorable mention is due. While her story is not told in a detailed narrative, her legacy is woven into the very fabric of Israel's priesthood and, ultimately, the coming of the Messiah. I am, of course, speaking of Elisheba, the wife of Aaron, the first high priest.

Elisheba's own heritage is noteworthy; she was a woman of the royal tribe of Judah, the daughter of Amminadab and sister of Nahshon, a prince of Judah. This union was profoundly significant, strategically marrying the leadership of the priestly line (Levi) with the future royal line (Judah), a symbolic prefiguring of the perfect King-Priest to come.

As Aaron's wife, Elisheba stood at the heart of the newly established priestly system. She bore him four sons: Nadab, Abihu, Eleazar, and Ithamar. Through these sons, she became the matriarch of the high priestly line, a dynasty that would serve Israel for generations. Her life, however, was marked by both divine honor and profound tragedy. She experienced the unimaginable grief of losing her two eldest sons, Nadab and Abihu, who were struck down by God for offering "strange fire" before the Lord—an act of unauthorized worship that violated sacred protocol (Leviticus 10:1-2). This catastrophic event underscores that the privilege of priesthood carried with it the gravest responsibility.

While the complete lineages of her sons are not fully detailed in scripture, we can trace a powerful thread of her legacy through her third son, Eleazar. Upon Aaron's death, Eleazar ascended to become the second High Priest of Israel. It was he who successfully passed the sacred mantle to his own son, Phinehas, who was zealously commended by God for his actions at Peor.

This priestly line, originating from Elisheba and Aaron, holds a breathtaking connection to the New Testament. We know with certainty that John the Baptist, the prophesied forerunner of Christ, was one of their direct descendants. Scripture explicitly confirms this by identifying John's mother, Elizabeth, as a "daughter of Aaron" (Luke 1:5). This phrase denotes her lineage, meaning she was a descendant of the tribe of Levi through the specific line of Aaron, not his literal daughter. Given the tragic end of Nadab and Abihu, who died without leaving heirs, and the noted continuation of the high priestly line through Eleazar and Ithamar, it is most likely that John the Baptist descended from Eleazar.

Therefore, Elisheba, this often-overlooked matriarch, serves as a crucial link in God's redemptive plan. Her bloodline flows from the tribe of Judah and merges with the priesthood of Levi, ultimately culminating centuries later in the voice crying in the wilderness—John the Baptist—who had the holy honor of preparing the way for the Lord Jesus Christ. We will, of course, explore the remarkable story of her descendant, Elizabeth, in the New Testament section of this book.

The Courageous Canaanite: Rahab

Our journey through the biblical narrative brings us now to the dramatic and foundational Book of Joshua, a text that chronicles the Israelites' entry into the Promised Land. It is here we will encounter one of scripture's most unexpected and courageous heroines. But before we step into her story, it is crucial to understand the complex historical backdrop of the book itself.

The authorship of Joshua is a subject of thoughtful scholarly debate. Ancient traditions, such as those preserved in the Babylonian Talmud, attribute the core of the book to Joshua ben Nun himself, with subsequent additions made by the High Priest Eleazar and his son, Phinehas. However, many modern biblical scholars view it through the lens of the "Deuteronomic History." This theory proposes that Joshua, along with Judges, Samuel, and Kings, was compiled and edited from a collection of earlier sources—perhaps including royal annals, victory songs, and eyewitness accounts—by inspired editors during the 7th and 6th centuries BC, a period of national reflection and reform. I ask you to hold this information in mind, as it becomes critically important to our understanding of the remarkable woman we are about to meet.

Our story picks up in Joshua Chapter 2. The great leader Joshua, having taken the mantle from Moses, sends two spies on a clandestine mission across the Jordan River to "view the land," with a specific focus on the formidable fortress city of Jericho. Their mission is one of reconnaissance: to assess the city's defenses and the morale of its people. Upon arriving in Jericho, seeking a place where their presence would attract the least suspicion, they find their way to the house of a woman named Rahab—a dwelling built into the city wall. And here, the text delivers a term that has caused a gross injustice to her character for millennia: it calls her a "harlot" (zônâ in Hebrew).

I am convinced this label could not be further from the truth. To understand why, we must look at the full biblical witness and the historical context. The Gospel of Matthew, in the very first chapter, provides a pivotal clue. In the genealogy of Jesus Christ, we find this listing: "Salmon the father of Boaz, whose mother was Rahab" (Matthew 1:5). This tells us two profound things: first, Rahab eventually married a man named Salmon, a prince of the tribe of Judah; second, she was honored as a direct ancestress of the Messiah, an incredible testament to her redeemed status and faith.

Now, consider the implications. Rahab was a wealthy Canaanite woman, The Bible tells us she had flax laid out on her roof (Joshua 2:6), a detail often overlooked. This indicates she was likely a successful merchant in the flax and linen trade, a lucrative business in that region. Her home, due to its location on the wall, probably also functioned as an inn or a tavern—a place where travelers and merchants could find lodging, conduct business, and receive news. As a wealthy, savvy, and independent businesswoman managing this enterprise, she would have frequently interacted with male patrons and clients, often under the cover of night to escape the daytime heat.

This is where we recall that earlier point about the book's authorship. A later Israelite editor, compiling stories from male soldiers or spies, would have looked upon this Canaanite woman living in a house on the wall, a woman of means who received unknown men at night, and made a natural—but incorrect—assumption based on his own cultural lens. The label zônâ was likely a misunderstanding of her profession, a smear born of prejudice, or perhaps even a strategic title used to explain why the spies would logically go to such a place without arousing immediate suspicion.

I stand firmly by this research. Rahab was not a woman of ill-repute; she was a courageous and honorable woman, a loving wife and mother, a shrewd business operator, and, as we will see, a person of profound and discerning faith. It is with this clarified vision of her true character that we can now fully appreciate the incredible strength and wisdom she displays in the rest of her story.

*****

The ancient, imposing walls of Jericho were a bastion of fear. For days, a palpable dread had settled over the city, a tension that thickened the air in the marketplace and hushed conversations in its homes. The cause of this terror was the rumored approach of the Israelite nation, a people whose God had famously parted the Red Sea and delivered crushing defeats to powerful kings. It was into this climate of anxiety that Joshua's two spies slipped, their mission to assess the fortifications and the morale of the city ahead of the impending Israelite assault.

Seeking a place that afforded both lodging and discreet observation, they found themselves at a house built into the very city wall itself—the residence of Rahab. This choice of location was likely strategic; her home, frequented by travelers and locals alike, provided a perfect cover for strangers to come and go without drawing immediate suspicion. They secured lodging, unaware that their entry had not gone entirely unnoticed. A keen eye, loyal to the king, had observed the foreign men and quickly reported their presence to the palace, branding them as obvious Israeli agents.

The response from the King of Jericho was swift and severe. A contingent of royal guards was dispatched to Rahab's door with a direct command: "Bring out the men who have come to you, who have entered your house, for they have come to search out all the country." The moment of crisis had arrived. With the king's soldiers at her threshold, Rahab faced an impossible choice: comply and betray her guests, or deceive the most powerful man in the city and risk a traitor's death.

With stunning composure, Rahab made her decision. She admitted to the royal officials that the men had indeed been there, a partial truth to lend credibility to her tale. She then woven a masterful deception: "Yes, the men came to me, but I did not know where they were from. And it happened as the gate was being shut, at dark, that the men went out. Where the men went I do not know; pursue them quickly, for you may overtake them." Her lie was not a simple denial but a calculated narrative designed to redirect the threat away from her home and out toward the fords of the Jordan River, buying precious time. What the king's men could not see was her breathtaking audacity—the two spies were not miles away, but mere feet above them, concealed beneath drying stalks of flax she had strategically laid out on her flat roof.

The king's men took the bait. Believing her story completely, they departed in haste, shutting the city gates behind them to prevent any escape, unknowingly sealing themselves in with the very spies they sought. The immediate danger had passed, but Rahab's role was far from over. She ascended to the roof and revealed to the hidden men the profound reason for her incredible risk. Her words, recorded in Joshua 2:9-13, are a remarkable confession of faith emerging from the most unexpected of places:

"I know that the LORD has given you the land," she began, "that the terror of you has fallen on us, and that all the inhabitants of the land are fainthearted because of you. For we have heard how the LORD dried up the water of the Red Sea for you when you came out of Egypt, and what you did to the two kings of the Amorites who were on the other side of the Jordan, Sihon and Og, whom you utterly destroyed. And as soon as we heard these things, our hearts melted; neither did there remain any more courage in anyone because of you, for the LORD your God, He is God in heaven above and on earth beneath."

This declaration is nothing short of astounding. Rahab, a Canaanite woman from a polytheistic culture steeped in idol worship, had not only heard the reports of Israel's God but had come to a stunning theological conclusion: Yahweh was the one true God of all creation. Her faith, born from hearing of His mighty acts, stood in stark contrast to the paralyzing fear that had gripped the rest of Jericho. While her city trembled at the power of the Israelites, Rahab alone revered the power of their God.

Having professed her belief, she then negotiated for her life and the lives of her family, extracting an oath from the spies: "Now therefore, I beg you, swear to me by the LORD, since I have shown you kindness, that you also will show kindness to my father's house, and give me a true token, and spare my father, my mother, my brothers, my sisters, and all that they have, and deliver our lives from death." The spies agreed, on one critical condition: to mark her house and ensure her family's safety, she must bind a scarlet cord in the same window through which she would later help them escape. Furthermore, her entire family must remain inside her house during the attack; anyone who left would be responsible for their own fate, but those who stayed would be under the spies' solemn protection.

Rahab quickly agreed to these terms. After ensuring the coast was clear, she let the men down the city wall with a rope from her window, advising them to hide in the hills for three days to avoid the king's search parties. True to her word, she immediately tied the scarlet cord in the window—a bold, public symbol of her faith and her covenant with the people of God. This crimson thread would become a sign of salvation for her household, a precursor to the Passover blood that spared the Israelites in Egypt.

The fulfillment of this oath is detailed in Joshua Chapter 6. When the walls of Jericho miraculously fell, Joshua honored the pledge, sending the same two spies into the devastation to escort Rahab and all her relatives to safety outside the camp of Israel. Scripture notes that "she dwells in Israel to this day," a testament to her full integration into the covenant community. Her legacy did not end there. She married Salmon, a prince of the tribe of Judah, and became the mother of Boaz—the nobleman who would redeem Ruth. Thus, this Canaanite woman, through her audacious faith and bravery, became the great-great-grandmother of King David and, centuries later, a named ancestor in the earthly lineage of Jesus Christ. While she fades from the main narrative, her courage echoes through salvation history, a timeless example of faith that transcends birthright and redefines destiny.

Warrior of Wisdom: Deborah

Before delving into the more famous narrative of Deborah, Israel's only woman Judge, the Book of Judges itself presents a foundational and formidable female figure in its very first chapter. This woman is Achsah, the daughter of Caleb ben Jephunneh . Her story, while technically first recorded in Joshua 15:16-19 as a historical footnote to the conquest of Canaan, is strategically retold in Judges 1:12-15, framing the entire era of the Judges with a powerful narrative of initiative and blessing.

The account begins with a classic warrior-hero trope. Caleb, now an elder and a legendary figure from Israel's past, offers a daring challenge: he will give his daughter Achsah's hand in marriage to the man who can capture the formidable Canaanite stronghold of Kirjath Sepher (the "City of Scribes," a place of both military and intellectual power in southern Canaan). The victor is Othniel, Caleb's own nephew, establishing him immediately as a man of exceptional courage and capability. Caleb, a man of unwavering integrity, honors his pledge, and Achsah and Othniel are married.

However, the story does not end with the hero winning his bride. It is here that Achsah transforms from a passive prize into the active protagonist. Recognizing that the land granted to her as a wedding gift—the Negev—was arid and difficult to cultivate, she understands that a field without water is a promise without a future. In a remarkable display of initiative, she first persuades her new husband to ask her father for a field. Caleb grants this request, but Achsah realizes it is not enough.

She then takes an audacious step that defies all convention. In Israelite society, daughters did not typically approach their fathers after marriage to ask for an additional inheritance; such matters of property and blessing were the domain of sons. Undeterred, Achsah deliberately and courageously approaches Caleb to ask for a blessing of a very specific kind: water rights. She understood that true prosperity in the promised land was tied not just to the soil, but to the life-giving resource that made it flourish. Achsah's courage and clarity were met with immense generosity. Impressed by her audacity and wisdom, Caleb bestowed upon her not just one spring, but a double blessing: the Upper Springs and the Lower Springs. This guaranteed a redundant and reliable water source for irrigation, transforming her arid land into a fertile and prosperous possession. Her actions ensured the economic viability and survival of her family's future.

This act of defiance was not disrespectful but brilliantly strategic. Achsah bravely broke with Hebrew tradition to secure the practical resources necessary for her family's future, demonstrating a wisdom that saw beyond immediate conquest to long-term sustainability. For this reason, modern scholars often refer to Achsah and Othniel as the Bible's first "power couple," and for good reason. Othniel, fueled by the stability and prosperity Achsah secured, goes on to become the first Judge of Israel, a deliverer who rescues the nation from oppression. This elevated position makes Achsah, in essence, the first "First Lady" of Israel—a woman of influence and stature in a nascent nation, long before the era of kings began. Her story, placed at the opening of Judges, serves as a powerful prelude: it is a narrative not just of military conquest, but of the cunning, wisdom, and assertive faith required to truly inhabit and thrive in the promised land.

*****

In the turbulent era of the Judges, a time characterized by a cyclical pattern of Israel's disobedience, foreign oppression, desperate cries for help, and divine rescue, we now turn to a uniquely brilliant dawn in Israel's history: the story of the prophetess Deborah.

Following the death of the previous judge, Ehud, the people of Israel had once again lapsed into doing evil in the sight of the LORD. In response, the Almighty sovereignly permitted their subjugation at the hands of a powerful and terrifying enemy: Jabin, the Canaanite king who reigned from the formidable fortress city of Hazor. His military commander was a man named Sisera, a name that would strike fear into the hearts of Israelites for two decades. The source of Jabin's overwhelming power was his fleet of nine hundred iron chariots—an ancient equivalent of an armored tank division—which made his army virtually unstoppable on the open plains. For twenty long years, the Israelites were ruthlessly oppressed, their spirits crushed, and their freedom extinguished.

It is into this landscape of fear and hopelessness that the narrative inserts a beacon of divine authority and wisdom: "Deborah, a prophetess, the wife of Lapidoth." She was not only the fourth and only female judge of Israel but a multifaceted leader. Her role transcended that of a mere arbitrator. She held court under a specific palm tree, known as "The Palm Tree of Deborah," situated between the towns of Ramah and Bethel in the mountainous region of Ephraim. This location became synonymous with justice and wisdom, as people from all over Israel would make the journey up into the mountains to have their disputes settled by her God-given discernment. She was not a ruler who commanded armies from a throne, but a motherly figure who delivered judgment from under a tree, earning her the reverent title, "the prophetess of the palm."

The narrative unfolds as we see her leadership spring into decisive action. She summons Barak, son of Abinoam, a military leader from Kedesh in Naphtali. The context suggests that God had already given a command to Barak and the Israelite forces through Deborah, but it had gone unheeded, likely due to the paralyzing fear of Sisera's chariots. Deborah's message to Barak is not a gentle suggestion but a powerful, rhetorical question meant to provoke him to faith and action: "Has not the LORD God of Israel commanded, 'Go and deploy troops at Mount Tabor; take with you ten thousand men of the sons of Naphtali and of the sons of Zebulun? And against you I will deploy Sisera, the commander of Jabin's army, with his chariots and his multitude at the River Kishon; and I will deliver him into your hand'?"

Barak's response reveals a profound crisis of courage. He does not doubt the message, but he doubts his own ability to execute it without the tangible presence of God's representative. He essentially conditions his obedience on Deborah's accompaniment, stating, "If you will go with me, then I will go; but if you will not go with me, I will not go!" Deborah, demonstrating her commitment to God's plan above all, agrees immediately. However, she prophesies a stunning consequence of his hesitation: "I will surely go with you; nevertheless, there will be no glory for you in the journey you are taking, for the LORD will sell Sisera into the hand of a woman." The honor of the final victory would be diverted from the military commander, a poignant blow in a patriarchal warrior culture.

At this point, the narrative strategically pauses to introduce a seemingly minor character: Heber the Kenite, who had separated from his clan and pitched his tent near the "terebinth tree at Zaanaim, which is beside Kedesh." This geographical note, which might appear incidental, is a masterful piece of storytelling foreshadowing, as Heber's family was on friendly terms with King Jabin.

The action escalates as Barak musters ten thousand men from Zebulun and Naphtali and ascends Mount Tabor as instructed. Word of this mobilization inevitably reaches Sisera in Harosheth-haggoyim. Confident in the superiority of his iron chariots, Sisera mobilizes his entire army and marches them toward the River Kishon, ready to crush the Israelite rebellion on the flat terrain where his chariots were dominant.

At the pivotal moment, with the massive Canaanite force arrayed below, Deborah delivers the divine signal to Barak: "Up! For this is the day in which the LORD has delivered Sisera into your hand. Has not the LORD gone out before you?" Emboldened by her faith, Barak leads his ten thousand men down the slopes of Mount Tabor. What happened next can only be attributed to the divine intervention Deborah had promised. The text states simply that "the LORD routed

Sisera and all his chariots and all his army." The precise method is not described, but ancient Jewish tradition and the song in Judges 5 suggest a sudden, torrential downpour that flooded the Kishon River, turning the plains into a bog of mud that immobilized the heavy iron chariots, making them useless and throwing the Canaanite army into a panic. Chaos ensued. Sisera, seeing his invincible war machine hopelessly mired, abandoned his chariot and fled on foot, leaving his entire army to be pursued and slaughtered by Barak's forces all the way back to their headquarters.

And here, the narrative circles back to Heber the Kenite. Sisera, fleeing for his life, ran directly toward the tent of Jael, Heber's wife, trusting in the alliance between Heber and King Jabin. Jael emerges from her tent to meet the exhausted and terrified commander. She masterfully disarms his suspicions with hospitality, inviting him in with the words, "Turn aside, my lord, turn aside to me; do not be afraid." She covers him with a rug to hide him. When he asks for water, she goes further, giving him nourishing milk, which would also induce sleep. Feeling secure, he commands her to stand guard at the tent entrance and deny his presence to any pursuers. As he fell into a deep, exhausted sleep, Jael took matters—and a tent peg and a hammer—into her own hands. In a breathtakingly bold and brutal act, she quietly approached the sleeping general and drove the tent peg through his temple, fastening his head to the ground.

Soon after, Barak arrived in hot pursuit. Jael went out to meet him as well and said, "Come, and I will show you the man whom you are seeking." He followed her into the tent and found Sisera lying dead, the instrument of his doom still piercing his skull. Thus, Deborah's prophecy was fulfilled to the letter: the glory of defeating the enemy commander went not to the warrior Barak, but to a woman.

This decisive victory broke the back of Canaanite power. The Israelites grew stronger and stronger until they eventually destroyed King Jabin himself. To commemorate this glorious deliverance, Deborah and Barak sang a powerful triumphal hymn recorded in Judges Chapter 5, a song that praises God as the ultimate warrior and celebrates the unlikely heroes—a mother in Israel and a tent-dwelling woman—whom He chose to use. The era of terror ended, and the land, once again, had rest for forty years.

The Nazerite's Mother

You may have noticed that the heading for this section is conspicuously unnamed, simply referring to her as "The Nazerite's Mother." This anonymity is a direct reflection of the biblical text in the Book of Judges, which, unlike many other pivotal matriarchs, never bestows upon her a personal name. We know her only through her relationships: she is the wife of Manoah, a man from the tribe of Gad, and she is historically significant as the fourth woman specifically cited in the Biblical narrative to suffer from barrenness, a condition often used in scripture to set the stage for a miraculous, God-ordained birth.

While the canonical Bible leaves her unnamed, Jewish tradition, as preserved in the Talmud, provides an identity for this important figure: Zelelponi (or Hazelelponi), a woman from the tribe of Judah. To honor this tradition and to provide a more personal and flowing narrative, we will henceforth refer to her by this name, Zelelponi.

The scripture gives no account of Zelelponi's age or how long she had endured the social and personal anguish of infertility. What it does provide is a profound and detailed account of the miracle that ended it. As described in Judges Chapter 13, the event began with a divine visitation: "And the Angel of the LORD appeared to the woman and said to her, 'Indeed now, you are barren and have borne no children, but you shall conceive and bear a son.'"

This announcement was immediately followed by a set of sacred prohibitions intended for Zelelponi herself. The angel instructed her to abstain completely from wine and strong drink and to avoid eating anything unclean, adhering to the strict dietary laws laid out in Leviticus Chapter 11. This was not merely for her health but to consecrate herself for the holy task of carrying a divinely appointed child.

The angel then revealed the extraordinary destiny of her unborn son: "Now therefore, please be careful not to drink wine or similar drink, and not to eat anything unclean. For behold, you shall conceive and bear a son. And no razor shall come upon his head, for the child shall be a Nazirite to God from the womb; and he shall begin to deliver Israel out of the hand of the Philistines." This meant her son was to be set apart for God under a Nazirite vow from the moment of conception, a lifelong commitment symbolized by his uncut hair, and his divine purpose would be to initiate Israel's liberation from its powerful Philistine oppressors.

Overwhelmed by this miraculous encounter and the stunning promise of a son and a savior, Zelelponi, in a fit of pure joy and awe, immediately sought out her husband, Manoah. After hearing her incredible story, a cautious yet faithful Manoah prayed to God, pleading for the angel to return to provide them with further guidance and confirmation. In His grace, God obliged.

The angelic messenger appeared once again to Zelelponi as she sat alone in a field. Recognizing him instantly, she hurried to fetch her husband. When Manoah arrived and heard the instructions firsthand—which closely mirrored what he had already told his wife—his response was one of ancient hospitality. He offered to prepare a young goat for the mysterious visitor to eat. The angel, however, politely declined the meal, redirecting the honor toward God. He suggested that if Manoah wished to make an offering, it should be a burnt offering presented to the LORD alone.

Acting on this, Manoah prepared the sacrifice upon a rock altar. What happened next was a spectacle of divine power that forever cemented the reality of their encounter: as the flames of their offering leapt toward heaven, the Angel of the LORD performed an impossible sign—he ascended dramatically into the sky within the very column of fire. Witnessing this breathtaking theophany, Manoah and Zelelponi fell prostrate, their faces to the ground in terror and worship.

In a moment of sheer panic, Manoah gasped to his wife, "We shall surely die, because we have seen God!" But it was Zelelponi who exhibited profound theological clarity and steady faith. She calmly and wisely reassured her husband, arguing that if God had intended to kill them, He would not have received their burnt offering, nor would He have revealed such an amazing promise to them or announced the imminent birth of their son. Her quick reasoning pacified Manoah's fear, redirecting their focus to the hope they had been given.

True to the divine word, Zelelponi soon conceived and bore a son, whom she named Samson. This child, set apart from the womb, would grow to become the most famous of the Nazirites and the last of the great Judges of Israel, using his God-given strength to begin the deliverance of his people from the Philistine menace, just as the angel had foretold.

The Philistine Betrayer: Delilah

In any literary or theological compendium dedicated to celebrating strong, courageous women and matriarchs, the disquieting inclusion of Delilah can initially strike the reader as a profound anomaly, a dissonant note in an otherwise harmonious symphony of female virtue and leadership. By the conventional metrics of such a work, her credentials are severely lacking. She was decidedly not a matriarch in the tradition of Sarah or Rebekah; she founded no dynasty, bore no child who would carry forth a covenant, and left no legacy of a faithful household. Her own lineage is shrouded in obscurity, with no mention of a noble or notable family, rendering her a woman without a past in a narrative world where genealogy is destiny. Most damningly, her identity is explicitly framed as that of a Philistine—a member of a people locked in perpetual, violent conflict with the Israelites, placing her squarely among the enemies of the very faith tradition this book seeks to honor.

Given this, her proximity to paragons like the faithfully resilient Sarah, the strategically astute Rebekah, the judicious and commanding prophetess Deborah, and the blessed mother Mary—the ultimate archetype of pious obedience—seems not just out of place, but almost subversive. One must therefore ask: what purpose does her dark and treacherous story serve in such company?

The answer lies not in emulation, but in examination. Her role, albeit brief and morally fraught, was critically important within the broader cosmological narrative of strength and weakness. Delilah's story provides an essential counterpoint, a masterclass in a different, more perilous kind of power—one rooted not in faith, wisdom, or nurture, but in relentless persuasion, sensual manipulation, and devastating betrayal. She stands as a stark cautionary tale, reminding us that formidable strength can be harnessed for destructive ends and that courage is not a virtue exclusive to the righteous. Her inclusion forces the reader to grapple with the complex, multifaceted nature of female influence, ensuring the conversation moves beyond simple hagiography into a more nuanced exploration of how women, in all their moral complexity, shape history. There are invaluable, albeit chilling, lessons to be learned from her story: the peril of misplaced trust, the seductive power of deception, and the sobering reality that the greatest threats often come not from obvious enemies on the battlefield, but from intimate adversaries in the quiet of one's own home.

*****

The tragic saga of Delilah unfolds in the Book of Judges, Chapter 16, a gripping narrative of betrayal, manipulation, and the fatal cost of misplaced trust. The stage is set with Samson, the divinely appointed Nazirite judge of Israel, whose prodigious strength is matched only by his profound weakness for Philistine women. Prior to meeting Delilah, his journey leads him to Gaza, a formidable stronghold of the Philistines. His purpose for entering enemy territory is telling: he seeks the company of a prostitute. While he is inside, his presence is discovered. The Gazites, seeing a prime opportunity to eliminate their archenemy, mobilize their forces. They secretly surround the entire city and set an ambush at its main gates, lying in wait through the night with the intent to kill him at first light.

Samson, however, is alerted to their plot. Rather than panic, he bides his time until the darkest hour—midnight. Then, in a breathtaking display of otherworldly power that confirms his status as more than a man, he approaches the city's main gate. Taking hold of the massive doors, the two towering doorposts, and the heavy crossbar that secured them, he tears the entire assembly from the stone wall. Placing the immense weight upon his shoulders, he carries this trophy of his invincibility up to the top of the hill that faces Hebron, a journey of nearly forty miles, leaving the humiliated Philistines in his wake.

At some point following this legendary feat, Samson's path leads him to the Valley of Sorek. It is here he encounters Delilah, a woman whose name would become synonymous with treachery. The text is silent on her origins, but she was likely a Philistine or a Canaanite living among them. Samson, once again governed by his desires, falls deeply in love with her.

His victory in Gaza made his capture the highest priority for the Philistine leadership. Recognizing his attachment to Delilah, the five lords of the Philistines—the rulers of Gaza, Ashkelon, Ashdod, Ekron, and Gath—personally approach her with a lucrative and sinister proposition. They entreat her to "entice" Samson and "see wherein his great strength lieth," promising to each pay her eleven hundred pieces of silver for the secret. This was an astronomical sum: a total of 5,500 silver shekels. To understand the magnitude of this bribe, it is a sum vastly greater than that for which Jesus was betrayed centuries later. Judas received thirty pieces of silver (Tyrian shekels); Delilah was offered the modern equivalent of over $110,000 USD, making the price on Samson's head—in purely monetary terms—far higher than that placed on the Messiah.

Seduced by this immense wealth, Delilah willingly becomes an agent of the state. She begins her campaign of manipulation, pleading with Samson to reveal the secret of his strength and how he might be bound and subdued. The great warrior, perhaps intoxicated by love or overconfident in his power, engages in a dangerous game. He lies to her, first claiming that binding him with seven fresh bowstrings, not yet dried, would render him helpless. The Philistines provided the cords, Delilah bound him, and Samson easily snapped them as if they were "threads of tow" touched by fire.

Undaunted and increasingly persistent, Delilah accused him of mocking her. He lied a second time, instructing her to use new ropes that had never been used. Again, she bound him, and again he broke free with ease. For a third deception, he told her weaving the seven locks of his hair into a web on a loom would capture his strength. Each time, Delilah enacted the falsehood, and each time Samson effortlessly broke the bonds, seemingly blind to the obvious pattern of betrayal unfolding in his own home.

Finally, Delilah shifted her tactic from enticement to emotional warfare. She wore him down with her words "daily," accusing him of a lack of trust and questioning his love for her. This constant nagging vexed his soul "unto death." Succumbing to this relentless pressure, the mighty Samson's resolve shattered. He revealed the sacred, Nazirite truth: no razor had ever come upon his head, for his strength was divinely ordained and resided in his consecrated hair.

Triumphant, Delilah sent for the Philistine lords. While Samson slept trustingly with his head in her lap, she had a man shave off the seven locks of his hair. For the first time in his life, his strength departed from him. He awoke to her cry, "The Philistines be upon thee, Samson!" but he, now "like any other man," was powerless. The Philistines seized him, gouged out his eyes, and bound him in bronze fetters, forcing him to grind grain in a prison in Gaza.

As for Delilah, having collected her blood money, she vanishes from the biblical narrative as abruptly as she entered it. Her ultimate fate remains a mystery, unknown whether she lived to enjoy her riches or perished later in the catastrophic destruction of the Dagon temple alongside the Philistine lords and the blinded—but ultimately redeemed—Samson. Her story endures as a stark and chilling lesson on the corrosive power of greed and the vulnerability of even the strongest to the betrayal of a trusted heart.

The Redeemed Moabite Woman: Ruth

Our journey now takes us to the book of Ruth, a precious gem nestled within the historical narratives of the Old Testament. Far more than a simple tale, it stands as one of scripture's most profound and endearing love stories—not merely romantic love, but the fierce, loyal love of covenant friendship, familial devotion, and ultimately, divine redemption.

To truly understand the heroine, Ruth, we must first meet the woman who shaped her destiny: Naomi. We are introduced to her in a time of deep distress, as a severe famine descends upon the promised land, specifically the region of Bethlehem in Judah. This "House of Bread" had become a house of lack, a poignant irony that sets the stage for a story of restoration. Driven by desperation to provide for his family, Naomi's husband, Elimelech, makes a fateful decision. He leads his wife and their two sons, Mahlon and Chilion, away from their ancestral inheritance in Judah to seek refuge in the pagan land of Moab—a nation historically at odds with Israel.

Settling in this foreign soil, the family's search for sustenance appears successful, but soon, tragedy strikes a devastating blow. Elimelech dies, leaving Naomi a widow in a hostile land, her sole comfort her two sons. As the years pass, the sons integrate further, marrying local Moabite women, Orpah and Ruth. The text, respecting the focus of the narrative, does not specify which son married which woman, unifying them in their shared experience as Naomi's daughters-in-law. For a decade, Naomi builds a life with this new family, only for catastrophe to strike again with unimaginable cruelty. Both Mahlon and Chilion also die, leaving Naomi utterly bereft—a childless widow in a foreign country, stripped of her protectors and her future, representing the most vulnerable class in the ancient world.

It is in this state of absolute desolation that Naomi receives a glimmer of hope: news that the Lord had visited His people in Judah, ending the famine and restoring the "House of Bread." With nothing left for her in Moab but bitter memories, Naomi resolves to return home. Setting out on the road with Orpah and Ruth, she is overcome by a sense of righteous obligation to these young women. In a moment of immense selflessness, she releases them from any duty to her. She kisses them and urges them to return to their mothers' homes in Moab, blessing them with a powerful benediction: "May the Lord deal kindly with you, as you have dealt with the dead and with me. May the Lord grant that you may find rest, each in the house of her husband." This blessing reveals a heart free of bitterness; Naomi holds no ill will and desires only prosperity and security for them, even if it means journeying on alone into her own grief.

Her words break open the floodgates of sorrow, and all three women weep openly, their bond so strong that the thought of parting is agony. In a desperate, heart-wrenching plea, Naomi argues with stark realism: even if she had hope of remarrying and bearing more sons that very night, could they possibly wait for them to grow up? The argument is absurd, and it finally convinces Orpah, who, after one last tearful kiss, turns back toward the familiar comfort of her pagan home.

But Ruth—Ruth clings to her. Naomi, perhaps believing Ruth acts out of obligation rather than conviction, points out that Orpah has made the sensible choice and tries once more to persuade her to leave. What happens next is one of the most beautiful and decisive declarations of commitment in all of scripture. Ruth's love for Naomi transcends duty; she loves her as her own mother. In response, she makes a sublime, seven-fold vow that forms the theological and emotional heart of the book:

"Do not urge me to leave you or to return from following you. For where you go I will go, and where you lodge I will lodge. Your people shall be my people, and your God my God. Where you die I will die, and there will I be buried. May the Lord do so to me and more also if anything but death parts me from you."

This is more than a promise; it is a comprehensive covenant of adoption. Ruth renounces her Moabite citizenship, her pagan gods, and her entire cultural identity to fully embrace Naomi's people, land, destiny, and—most significantly—Naomi's God, YHWH. It is a total life transformation sealed with a seven-fold promise, a number signifying divine perfection and completeness in scripture. This places Ruth's pledge on a monumental scale, echoing the gravity of God's covenant with Abram.

Seeing the unshakeable resolve in Ruth's spirit, Naomi finally ceases her arguments. She concedes in silence, and the two widows—one broken by grief yet accompanied by unwavering love—turn their faces toward Judah and journey on together, arriving in Bethlehem just as the barley harvest begins, a symbol of new beginnings and the providence that was guiding their every step.

*****

Having found a precarious new home in Bethlehem, the reality of their situation pressed heavily upon Ruth and Naomi. They were two widows alone, without a provider, and the bread in their cupboard would not last. Driven by a fierce, protective love for her mother-in-law and a resolute will to survive, Ruth took the initiative. She approached Naomi with a practical, yet humble, request: "Let me go to the field and glean among the ears of grain behind someone in whose sight I may find favor."

It is crucial to understand Ruth's motivation. She was not, at this initial stage, seeking a husband or a romantic entanglement. Her hope was far more immediate and noble—she sought the charitable permission of a landowner to follow his harvesters, gathering the stray stalks and dropped heads of barley they left behind. This was the provision Mosaic law made for the poor and the foreigner (Leviticus 19:9-10), and it was this mere sustenance that Ruth sought to secure for herself and Naomi.

Naomi, recognizing the necessity of the task, gave her weary consent. "Go, my daughter," she said. And so, Ruth set out for the fields, joining the nameless poor who trailed the harvest crews, a picture of vulnerability and determination.

The narrative then unveils a divinely orchestrated coincidence: the field she chose to enter belonged to a man named Boaz, who was from the clan of Elimelech, Naomi's deceased husband. This detail, a masterful piece of foreshadowing, plants the seed for the redemption that is to come.

The rhythms of the harvest were well underway when Boaz, a man of substance and integrity, arrived from Bethlehem. His practiced eye scanned the work of his reapers, and it was then that he noticed a new figure among the gleaners—a young woman whose diligent work and unfamiliar face set her apart. He inquired of his foreman, "Whose young woman is that?"

The servant overseeing the workers clarified her identity, offering not just her name but her remarkable story. "She is the Moabite young woman who came back with Naomi from the country of Moab. And she said, 'Please let me glean and gather among the sheaves after the reapers.' So she came, and she has continued from early morning until now, except for a short rest in the shelter."

This report sets the stage for their first recorded interaction. Moved by what he had heard, Boaz approached Ruth directly. His instructions to her were not commands of control, but profound acts of protection and provision. "Listen, my daughter," he began, a term of endearing respect. "Do not go to glean in another field, and do not leave this one. Stick close to my young women. Keep your eyes on the field they are reaping and follow after them. I have charged the young men not to touch you." He then extended his kindness to her most basic needs: "And when you are thirsty, go to the vessels and drink what the young men have drawn."

Ruth, overwhelmed by this unexpected and generous patronage from a man of his stature, fell facedown in a posture of profound gratitude and humility. "Why have I found such favor in your eyes," she asked, "that you should take notice of me, since I am a foreigner?"

Boaz's response reveals that his kindness was a direct result of her renowned character. He said, "All that you have done for your mother-in-law since the death of your husband has been fully told to me, and how you left your father and mother and your native land and came to a people that you did not know before." He had not just seen a hard worker; he had seen a woman of exemplary loyalty and courage. He then pronounced a blessing over her, invoking the God she had chosen to serve: "The LORD repay you for what you have done, and a full reward be given you by the LORD, the God of Israel, under whose wings you have come to take refuge!"

The interaction culminated with Ruth acknowledging the deep comfort of his words. "May I continue to find favor in your eyes, my lord, for you have comforted me and spoken kindly to your servant, though I am not one of your servants." She had indeed already found that favor.

At the mealtime, Boaz's extraordinary kindness continued. He broke from social convention by inviting her to not just eat apart, but to join him and his workers. "Come here," he said, "and eat some bread and dip your morsel in the wine." He served her parched grain himself, a gesture of honor and inclusion. In a moment that defines her selfless character,

Ruth ate what she needed but deliberately set aside a portion of her meal to take back to Naomi.

After the meal, Boaz instructed his men to go even further beyond the requirements of gleaning laws. He ordered them to intentionally let grain fall from their bundles for her to gather, and to even allow her to glean directly from the bound sheaves themselves—an act of generosity that was virtually unheard of, effectively making her a member of the harvesting crew. He sternly warned the young men not to rebuke her, ensuring her safety and dignity.

Ruth labored in this privileged space until evening, then diligently threshed the barley she had gathered to separate the valuable grain from the worthless chaff. The yield was staggering: an ephah of barley, a volume equivalent to nearly 50 pounds of flour—an amount far beyond what any typical gleaner could hope to collect, enough to sustain both women for many days.

She returned to Naomi in the city, presenting her with the saved portion of her meal and the immense bounty of grain. Naomi, astonished, blessed the unknown benefactor and asked, "Where did you glean today? Where did you work? Blessed be the man who took notice of you."

When Ruth revealed the name of her patron—"The man's name with whom I worked today is Boaz"—Naomi's eyes were opened to the divine hand at work. She recognized the name instantly and exclaimed, "May he be blessed by the LORD, whose kindness has not forsaken the living or the dead! That man is a close relative of ours, one of our redeemers." Understanding the safety this connection provided, Naomi advised Ruth, "It is good, my daughter, that you go out with his young women, lest in another field you be assaulted." Ruth heeded this wise counsel, and she continued to glean alongside Boaz's servant women until the conclusion of both the barley and wheat harvests, secure under the protective and growing favor of Boaz.

*****

With the final grains of the harvest stored away and the bustling activity of the fields replaced by a hushed expectancy, a palpable tension settled over the small house of Naomi. The provision from the barley and wheat harvests was a temporary relief, but for two vulnerable widows in ancient Bethlehem, long-term security was a matter of survival. Seeing the precariousness of their situation, the aging Naomi, once embittered by loss but now galvanized by a fierce, protective love for her devoted daughter-in-law, resolved to act. She would leverage the sacred customs of their people to secure a future for Ruth.

Knowing the law of the kinsman-redeemer (go'el), which charged a nearest relative with the duty of preserving a deceased man's lineage and property, Naomi's thoughts turned to Boaz. He was not only a man of immense wealth and sterling reputation but also, as she reminded Ruth with a glimmer of strategic hope, "one of our close relatives." This was their God-given loophole, their chance at redemption.

With the precision of a general deploying her most valuable agent, Naomi outlined a daring plan to Ruth. Her instructions were specific, symbolic, and fraught with risk, designed to navigate the delicate balance between boldness and propriety. "Therefore," Naomi began, her voice low and earnest, "wash yourself and anoint yourself with oil—not as for a festival, but as a bride preparing for her wedding night. Put on your best garment, the one that speaks of dignity, not allure. Then, under the cover of darkness, go down to the threshing floor where Boaz will be winnowing his barley and spending the night to guard his harvest."

Understanding the immense vulnerability this would entail, Naomi's counsel was crucially cautious. "But do not make yourself known to the man until he has finished eating and drinking and has lain down for the night. Let his contentment and sleep make him receptive. Then, note carefully the place where he lies. You are to go in quietly, uncover his feet—a gesture of submission and a request for protection—and lie down at his feet. From that position of humility, he will tell you what you should do."

To Naomi's immense relief and pride, Ruth, the Moabitess who had clung to her and her God, agreed without a moment's hesitation. "All that you say to me I will do," she vowed, her faith in Naomi's wisdom and in the God of Israel outweighing any fear.

That night, Ruth followed the instructions to the letter. The threshing floor, usually a place of labor, was now a scene of intimate drama under a canopy of stars. As Boaz slept, content from his meal, Ruth quietly moved. She gently turned back the corner of his cloak, exposing his feet to the night air, and lay down. Hours later, Boaz stirred in the cold, turning over in his sleep, and was startled to find a woman lying at his feet in the dark. "Who are you?" he demanded, his voice a mixture of sleep and alarm.

Ruth's response was perfectly crafted, a declaration of both identity and intent: "I am Ruth, your maidservant." Then, she took the courageous step, invoking the law of the kinsman-redeemer: "Take your maidservant under your wing, for you are a close relative." She was asking not for a clandestine affair, but for the protection of marriage and the perpetuation of Elimelech's line.

Boaz's shock melted into profound respect and blessing. "Blessed are you of the LORD, my daughter!" he exclaimed. "For you have shown more kindness at the end than at the beginning." He recognized that her actions were not those of a young woman seeking romance or wealth; she could have pursued younger men, whether poor or rich. Instead, she was fulfilling her duty to Naomi's family with loyalty and virtue. "And now, my daughter," he reassured her, "do not fear. I will do for you all that you request, for all the people of my town know that you are a virtuous woman."

Yet, honor demanded he navigate the law precisely. "It is true that I am a close relative," Boaz confirmed, "however, there is a relative closer than I." He promised to approach this man in the morning, offering him the right of redemption first. To ensure her safety and reputation, he instructed her to remain with him in the protective seclusion of the threshing floor until just before dawn, when she could return home unseen.

As the first hints of light touched the horizon, Boaz ensured her return was not only discreet but also provisioned. He loaded her shawl with a massive gift—six ephahs of barley, a symbol of his willingness to provide and a promise of his intent. His instruction to not be seen was not born of shame, but was a final, careful act of guardianship, protecting her virtue from any potential gossip or misunderstanding.

Ruth returned to a waiting Naomi, who greeted her with an anxious, "Is that you, my daughter?" Ruth poured out the entire story and presented the heavy bundle of barley—tangible evidence of Boaz's generosity. The older woman, wise in the ways of men and God, interpreted the signs perfectly. The gift was a message; it was a pledge. With calm certainty, Naomi reassured Ruth, "Wait, my daughter, until you learn how the matter turns out, for the man will not rest until he has concluded the matter this very day." The wheels of redemption had been set in motion, and they now placed their hope in the honor of Boaz.

*****

Following through on his promise to Ruth, Boaz, a man of integrity and strategic mind, immediately set his plan into motion. His first task was to locate the nearer kinsman-redeemer, the man who, by the strict letter of the law, held the prior right and responsibility to redeem the land of Naomi's late husband, Elimelech.

Understanding the man's character, Boaz chose his words with the precision of a master strategist. He knew that avarice was the lever he could pull to achieve a righteous end. He organized a formal meeting at the city gate, the ancient equivalent of a town square and courthouse, where all legal and communal business was conducted. There, he first summoned the relative and then called upon ten of the city's elders to serve as official witnesses, ensuring the proceedings would be legally binding and publicly unquestionable.

Before the assembled elders, Boaz began his carefully constructed proposal. He started not with the complication of Ruth, but with the attraction of the land. "My friend," he said, "Naomi, who has returned from Moab, is selling a piece of land that belonged to our relative Elimelech. I thought I should bring it to your attention and suggest that you buy it in the presence of these respected witnesses." He paused, letting the prospect of a valuable new acquisition sink in. "If you wish to redeem it, do so. But if not, tell me so I will know, for I am next in line after you."

Just as Boaz had anticipated, the man's eyes lit up with the prospect of a profitable deal. Without a second thought for any hidden obligations, his greed propelled him forward. "All right, I'll redeem it!" he declared hastily, seizing what he believed was an opportunity for personal gain.

This was the crucial moment. With the man's commitment publicly secured, Boaz unveiled the full, binding condition of the redemption. "Of course," Boaz continued, his voice calm and deliberate, "on the day you buy the land from Naomi, you also acquire Ruth the Moabite, the widow of the dead man. This is so that her first son will carry on her late husband's name and keep the inheritance within the family."

The effect was immediate and devastating. The kinsman-redeemer's confident demeanor crumbled. The land, once a coveted asset, was now transformed into a liability. To marry Ruth meant not only sharing the inherited wealth with potential future sons who would not be his own heirs but also diluting his own family's estate. His greed, which had moments before been his driving force, now became his undoing. "Then I cannot redeem it," he backpedaled, a note of panic in his voice. "Doing so would jeopardize my own inheritance. You redeem the land; I cannot do it."

To formalize his relinquishment of the right, he performed the ancient customary ritual. He took off his sandal and handed it to Boaz. This public act, done before the witnesses, was a legally recognized symbol of the transfer of rights and responsibilities.

The elders, who had observed the entire exchange, immediately affirmed the transaction. They declared, "We are witnesses!" and proceeded to pronounce a profound blessing upon Boaz and Ruth, invoking the names of the great matriarchs Rachel and Leah, and praying that Boaz's house would be as prosperous and significant as that of Perez, the son of Tamar and Judah—an ancestor who himself was the product of another courageous story of preservation.

True to the agreement and his own heart, Boaz took Ruth as his wife. The Lord blessed their union, and she soon bore a son. The women of the town rejoiced with Naomi, who had once returned from Moab bitter and empty. They praised God for providing a goel, a redeemer, for her family. "May this child be famous in Israel!" they cried. "He will renew your life and sustain you in your old age, for your daughter-in-law who loves you—who is better to you than seven sons—has given him birth!"

In a deeply moving scene of restoration, Naomi, whose arms had been empty of sons and grandchildren, now cuddled the infant to her breast, becoming his nursemaid and loving him as if he were her own. The community's blessing of fame was prophetic, though they could not have known its full scope. The boy was named Obed. While Obed himself would not achieve renown, his lineage would redefine history. He would father a son named Jesse, and Jesse would father a son named David—the shepherd boy who would become Israel's greatest king and the earthly ancestor of the ultimate Redeemer.

The Book of Ruth Study Guide

Background and Introduction:

The story of Ruth takes place in the time of the judges (after the conquest of Canaan and before 1050 BC). No author is named, but according to Jewish verbal tradition, the Prophet Samuel wrote it. The overarching theme in Ruth is the kinsman redeemer, to understand what that law is let's go to Deuteronomy 25:5-10

5 "If brothers dwell together, and one of them dies and has
no son, the widow of the dead man shall not be *married* to a
stranger outside *the family;* her husband's brother shall go in
to her, take her as his wife, and perform the duty of a
husband's brother to her. **6** And it shall be *that* the firstborn
son which she bears will succeed to the name of his dead
brother, that his name may not be blotted out of Israel. **7** But
if the man does not want to take his brother's wife, then let
his brother's wife go up to the gate to the elders, and say, 'My
husband's brother refuses to raise up a name to his brother
in Israel; he will not perform the duty of my husband's
brother.' **8** Then the elders of his city shall call him and speak
to him. But *if* he stands firm and says, 'I do not want to take
her,' **9** then his brother's wife shall come to him in the
presence of the elders, remove his sandal from his foot, spit
in his face, and answer and say, 'So shall it be done to the
man who will not build up his brother's house.' **10** And his

name shall be called in Israel, 'The house of him who had his sandal removed.'

Chapter 1:
The Country of Moab was founded by Lot's son Moab Gen 19:37 making the Moabite peoples cousins of the Israelites
Elimelech means "God is King" & Naomi means "pleasantness" or "delight".
Ruth means "Compassionate Companion"

1:16-17 The 7 fold promise

1: Where you go I will Go
2: Where you lodge I will lodge
3: Your people will be my People
4: Your God will be My God
5: Where you did I will die
6: And there will I be buried
7: May the Lord punish me severely if I allow anything but death to separate us!
The number 7 in Biblical numerology is associated with Perfection and Completeness, Ruth is the first and only mortal person in the bible to use a 7 fold promise.

God gives one to Abraham in Gen 12:2-3
Jesus gives on to his disciples in Matt 5:1-9
And Jesus gives one to the Church in Rev chapter 2

Mara means bitter

Chapter 2:

Boaz means Swiftness or Swift

Boaz is the son of Salmon and Rahab Matt 1:4
Rahab is known for her role in the book of Joshua when she helped hide the spies on the roof of her linen shop. She was not a prostitute even though it is written in the bible, remember Joshua was written as a report to Joshua about the events of Jericho as a record for Joshua to keep. Whoever wrote it saw Rahab as an independently wealthy woman and assumed she earned her wealth by way of promiscuous work as most women of the day did. Rahab was happily married and as virtuous as Ruth.
An honorable mention is Boaz's 6th Great grandmother Tamar from Gen chapter 38.
She pretended to be a prostitute and seduced Judah thus conceiving twins Perez and Zerah.

To glean means to simply pick up barley grain that has fallen to the ground.

Epah = 30-40 pounds or about half a bushel.

Chapter 4

Obed means Servant of God

Jesse means Gift

David means Beloved

The Prophet’s Mother: Hannah

Our journey through the Biblical narrative brings us to a pivotal and deeply human drama in the first book of Samuel. Here, we encounter the fifth and final barren woman in a significant lineage that includes Sarah, Rebekah, Rachel, and Samson's mother. This woman is Hannah, whose story is not just one of personal heartbreak, but a crucial turning point in the history of Israel.

We are introduced to the setting: a man named Elkanah, a devout Levite from the hill country of Ephraim, who made an annual pilgrimage to the tabernacle at Shiloh to worship and sacrifice to the Lord. His family life, however, was marked by profound tension. Like several patriarchs before him, he had two wives: Peninnah, who had given him children, and Hannah, whom he loved deeply but who remained childless. In the ancient Near East, a woman's value and security were intrinsically linked to her ability to bear sons. Barrenness was not merely a personal sorrow but a social stigma, often seen as a sign of divine disfavor.

This cultural context fuels the conflict. Peninnah, perhaps jealous of Elkanah's clear preference for Hannah, weaponized her rival's barrenness. The scripture paints her as a cruel adversary who would deliberately "provoke her severely, to make her miserable" because the Lord had closed Hannah’s womb. This was not a one-time slight but a relentless, annual torment. Every year, during what should have been a sacred and joyful festival, Peninnah's taunts would reduce Hannah to tears and despair. The situation was exacerbated during the sacrificial meal. Out of his great love for her, Elkanah would give Hannah a double portion of the sacrificial meat, a tender but ultimately misguided gesture that highlighted her unique status and, by contrast, her painful deficiency—she had no children to share it with.

Elkanah, though well-intentioned, failed to grasp the depth of his wife's anguish. Seeing her weep and refuse food, he would try to comfort her with logic: "Hannah, why do you weep? Why do you not eat? And why is your heart grieved? Am I not better to you than ten sons?" While his words stemmed from love, they could not soothe a maternal longing that he, as a father, could never fully understand. His presence, however cherished, was not a substitute for the child she yearned for.

Finally, after years of enduring this cycle of humiliation and grief, Hannah reached a breaking point. During one pilgrimage, overwhelmed with heartbreak, she rose from the meal and stumbled to the tabernacle to pour out her soul in desperate prayer. She "wept in anguish" and made a radical, irrevocable vow to the Lord of Heaven's Armies. Her prayer was a profound bargain born of deep faith: "O Lord of hosts, if You will indeed look on the affliction of Your maidservant and remember me, and not forget Your maidservant, but will give Your maidservant a male child, then I will give him to the Lord all the days of his life, and no razor shall ever come upon his head." This vow is extraordinarily significant. By dedicating her potential son to God for life and vowing that no razor would touch his head, she was effectively pledging him as a Nazirite—a person set apart for God's service under a strict vow, as detailed in Numbers Chapter 6. This placed her son in the same consecrated category as the great judge Samson, hinting that her child was destined for a monumental purpose.

In her grief, Hannah prayed silently, her lips moving but her voice unheard. The high priest, Eli, was sitting at his post by the doorpost of the temple. Observing her strange behavior, he jumped to a shameful conclusion: he accused her of being drunk and disgracefully coming before the Lord in such a state. "How long will you be drunk? Put your wine away from you!" he scolded.

Hannah, though unjustly accused, responded with remarkable humility and grace. She corrected him gently but firmly: "No, my lord, I am a woman of sorrowful spirit. I have drunk neither wine nor intoxicating drink, but have poured out my soul before the Lord. Do not consider your maidservant a wicked woman, for out of the abundance of my complaint and grief I have spoken until now." Her dignified response moved Eli. Recognizing his error and her genuine piety, he transformed from accuser to benefactor, offering a priestly blessing: "Go in peace, and the God of Israel grant your petition which you have asked of Him."

These words were a balm to Hannah's wounded spirit. Faith surged within her. She thanked Eli, returned to her family, her countenance utterly transformed. For the first time in years, she was able to eat, and her sadness lifted, replaced by a peaceful hope. The following morning, they worshipped and returned to their home in Ramah.

True to His nature, the Lord remembered Hannah. In due time, she conceived and bore a son. She named him Samuel (שמואל / Shmu'el), a name that sounds like "heard by God" or "God has heard," serving as a perpetual testament to answered prayer.

When the next year's sacrifice arrived, Hannah made a difficult but faithful decision. She would not go up to Shiloh until the boy was weaned—a process that likely took three to four years in that culture. She explained to Elkanah that she must stay to nurse her son so that when she did present him at the temple, he could "remain there forever." Elkanah supported her vow.

When the time finally came, Hannah journeyed to Shiloh with her young son, along with a three-year-old bull, a measure of flour, and a skin of wine for a lavish sacrifice of dedication. She approached Eli and reminded him of their encounter years prior: "O my lord! As your soul lives, my lord, I am the woman who stood by you here, praying to the Lord. For this child I prayed, and the Lord has granted me my petition which I asked of Him. Therefore I also have lent him to the Lord; as long as he lives he shall be lent to the Lord."

With this, she left her young son in Eli's care to begin his life of service at the tabernacle. The narrative then treats us to Hannah's Song (1 Samuel 2:1-10), a magnificent psalm of praise that exalts God for reversing human fortunes, lifting up the humble, and shattering the strength of the proud. This song echoes through the ages, finding its ultimate fulfillment in the Magnificat of Mary, the mother of Jesus.

Hannah's love for Samuel did not end with her sacrifice. Scripture tenderly notes that each year she would make a little robe for him and bring it when the family came for the annual sacrifice. And God, in His abundant grace, did not leave Hannah with an empty home. He blessed her further, giving her three more sons and two daughters, ensuring her legacy and security. Meanwhile, the boy Samuel grew up in the presence of the Lord, and would go on to become the last and greatest of Israel's judges, a mighty prophet, and the man chosen to anoint Israel's first two kings, Saul and David, shaping the very destiny of the nation.

Noteworthy Mentions: 1&2 Samuel, 1 Kings

An Exploration of Notable Women in the Deuteronomistic History

The narrative tapestry of 1 & 2 Samuel, 1 & 2 Kings, and 1 & 2 Chronicles is often dominated by the political and military exploits of kings, priests, and prophets. However, woven into this grand narrative are the stories of pivotal women whose actions, both direct and indirect, profoundly shaped the destiny of the Israelite monarchy. This section will explore these often-overlooked figures, examining their roles not merely as wives and daughters, but as political pawns, agents of prophecy, and crucial links in the messianic lineage.

1 Samuel: Women in the Courts of Saul and David

The book of 1 Samuel introduces the first kings of Israel, and the women surrounding them were central to establishing and challenging royal authority.

Ahinoam, daughter of Ahimaaz: As the wife of King Saul, Ahinoam holds the significant but shadowy title of the first Queen of Israel. While the text provides scant detail about her character, her presence establishes the institution of the royal household. She is the mother of several of Saul's children, including his esteemed son Jonathan and his daughters Merab and Michal, thus rooting the Saulide dynasty. Her existence is often noted in contrast to David's own wife, who also bore the name Ahinoam, creating a symbolic rivalry between the two royal houses.

Merab, King Saul's Oldest Daughter: Merab's story is one of political bargaining. Saul initially promises Merab to David as a reward for his military prowess against the Philistines, viewing the marriage as a "snare" to entrap David by forcing him into greater military dangers to earn his bride (1 Samuel 18:17). However, Saul reneges on his promise and gives her to Adriel of Meholath instead. This act of betrayal not only highlights Saul's duplicity but also serves to further alienate David from the king. Her fate is tragically tied to Saul's downfall; later, five of her sons are handed over to the Gibeonites and executed to atone for Saul's past crimes (2 Samuel 21:8).

Michal, King Saul's Younger Daughter: Michal is one of the most dynamic and tragic female figures in the Bible. Her story is a complex blend of loyalty, love, and heartbreaking alienation. Unlike her sister, Michal is explicitly said to love David (1 Samuel 18:20). She actively saves David's life by helping him escape through a window from her father's assassins, and she tricks Saul's messengers by placing a household idol in his bed. After being given to another man, Paltiel, she is forcibly returned to David to solidify his political claim to Saul's throne. Her story culminates in a bitter rupture with David when she criticizes him for dancing with unrestrained joy before the Ark of the Covenant, revealing a deep cultural and spiritual rift between the daughter of the first king and the passionate David. The poignant note that "Michal daughter of Saul had no children to the day of her death" (2 Samuel 6:23) is not merely a biological detail but a profound theological statement, signifying the end of Saul's direct lineage and the irrevocable transfer of the royal line to David.

2 Samuel: Bathsheba and the Consequences of Power

The central and most famous woman in 2 Samuel is Bathsheba. Her story is a critical turning point in the narrative of King David, marking his descent from a heroic "man after God's own heart" to a flawed ruler susceptible to corruption.

The text introduces her not by name, but as "the wife of Uriah the Hittite," a loyal soldier in David's army. David, from his palace roof, sees her bathing and, driven by lust and the assumption of royal prerogative, summons her. Their adultery results in a pregnancy. David's subsequent attempts to cover his sin escalate into a grave abuse of power: he recalls Uriah from the front lines, hoping he will sleep with his wife and believe the child is his. When Uriah's profound loyalty to his fellow soldiers prevents this, David orchestrates his murder by sending him to the fiercest part of the battle and withdrawing support.

From Victim to Queen Mother: While initially presented as a passive figure in the transgression, Bathsheba's role evolves. After Uriah's death and her period of mourning, she becomes David's wife. The prophet Nathan directly confronts David for his sin, and the child conceived from the adultery dies. However, their next son, Solomon, is loved by God (2 Samuel 12:24-25). Bathsheba later plays a crucial active role in securing the throne for Solomon when David is old and infirm, shrewdly navigating the court politics to ensure his succession (1 Kings 1:15-31).

Messianic Significance: Bathsheba's ultimate importance is solidified in the genealogical record. She is listed explicitly in the Gospel of Matthew as the wife of Uriah and mother of Solomon (Matthew 1:6), making her a direct ancestor of Jesus Christ. Furthermore, through her son Nathan (mentioned in Luke's genealogy, Luke 3:31), she is also an ancestor of the Virgin Mary, placing her at the root of both legal and biological lines of the Messiah.

1 Kings: Naamah and the Division of a Kingdom

In 1 Kings, the focus shifts to Solomon's reign and its aftermath. A key figure in this transition is Naamah.

The Ammonite Queen Mother: Naamah is identified as an Ammonite, making her a foreign wife—a fact the Deuteronomistic historians would have viewed with suspicion, as Solomon's marriages to foreign women for political alliances ultimately led him into idolatry (1 Kings 11:1-8). Despite this, her significance is undeniable.

Mother of Rehoboam: Naamah was the mother of Rehoboam (Roboam), Solomon's son and successor. It was Rehoboam's foolish and heavy-handed policies that directly caused the northern ten tribes of Israel to revolt, permanently splitting the united monarchy into the separate kingdoms of Israel (north) and Judah (south). Thus, as the mother of the king who presided over the fracturing of the kingdom, Naamah occupies a pivotal place in biblical history.

Continued Messianic Line: Despite the disaster of the schism, the Davidic line continued through Rehoboam in the kingdom of Judah. This means Naamah, a foreign queen mother, became a crucial link in preserving the lineage that would eventually lead to Christ, as detailed in the genealogy of Matthew 1:7.

The Painted Queen: Jezebel

While we journey through the narrative of 1st Kings, we encounter a figure whose very name has transcended the biblical text to become a universal byword for wickedness: Queen Jezebel. Her infamy is so deeply embedded in our cultural lexicon that to label someone a "Jezebel"—or to accuse them of having "the spirit of Jezebel"—is to invoke a powerful and damning accusation of manipulation, moral corruption, and brazen defiance.

This label is often applied, sometimes carelessly, in modern contexts, particularly toward women. It is frequently directed at young women who defy conservative social norms—those who wear what is deemed too much makeup, dress in a manner perceived as overtly sexual or promiscuous, or who exhibit a confident, assertive, and unapologetic demeanor.

However, as we delve into the authentic, historical narrative of Jezebel found in 1st Kings, we will uncover the profound and terrifying reasons this specific Queen's name, above all others, became the archetype for a particular kind of evil. Her story is not one of mere personal vanity or seduction, but of a vast and systematic campaign of state-sponsored idolatry, the brutal persecution of God's prophets, the ruthless manipulation of power through forgery and murder, and a chilling, unrepentant pride that challenged divine authority itself. By examining her actions—from introducing the worship of Baal and Asherah to orchestrating the wrongful seizure of Naboth's vineyard—we will begin to understand the true nature of the "spirit of Jezebel." It is a spirit of controlling ideology, tyrannical power, and the active, aggressive attempt to eradicate faith and conscience, which provides a much darker and more complex foundation for her enduring legacy.

*****

Jezebel's introduction into the biblical narrative is both precise and portentous. She is first mentioned in 1 Kings 16:31 not merely as a new queen, but as a transformative and ominous political force: "And it came to pass, as though it had been a trivial thing for him to walk in the sins of Jeroboam the son of Nebat, that Ahab took as wife Jezebel the daughter of Ethbaal, king of the Sidonians; and he went and served Baal and worshiped him." This single verse establishes her not just as King Ahab's wife, but as the catalyst for a state-sponsored religious revolution in the northern kingdom of Israel. As a princess of Sidon (a powerful Phoenician city-state), her marriage to Ahab was a strategic alliance, but she arrived as a zealous missionary for her pagan deities, Baal and Asherah, effectively importing her court and her gods into the heart of Samaria.

The gravity of her influence is immediately underscored at the opening of 1 Kings 18. The chapter begins with God instructing the prophet Elijah to present himself to King Ahab to end a severe, three-year famine that God Himself had decreed as judgment against Israel's idolatry. Simultaneously, Ahab summons his palace administrator, Obadiah, to scour the land for any remaining pasture. The narrative then reveals the terrifying reality of Jezebel's reign: she had been systematically slaughtering the prophets of the

Lord. Obadiah, a devout man who feared God greatly, risked his own life by hiding one hundred prophets in caves and secretly sustaining them with bread and water. Thus, Jezebel's story begins against a backdrop of divine judgment (famine), prophetic confrontation (Elijah), and ruthless religious persecution directed by the queen herself.

Before the confrontation directly involves Jezebel, the narrative pivots to one of the most dramatic displays of divine power in the Old Testament: the contest on Mount Carmel. Empowered by God, Elijah instructs Obadiah to fetch Ahab and then commands the king to gather all Israel and the 850 prophets of Baal and Asherah "who eat at Jezebel's table"—a explicit detail highlighting that these pagan priests were state employees, funded and protected by the queen. Before the assembled nation, Elijah issues a stark ultimatum: "How long will you falter between two opinions? If the Lord is God, follow Him; but if Baal, follow him." The people are silent, paralyzed by indecision.

Elijah then proposes a definitive test. Two bulls are prepared for sacrifice on two altars, but no fire is to be lit. The prophets of Baal are to call on their god, and Elijah will call on the Lord; the deity who answers by consuming the sacrifice with fire is the one true God. The prophets of Baal pray, dance, and ecstatically shout from morning until noon with no result. Elijah, with sharp sarcasm, mocks their efforts: "Cry aloud, for he is a god; either he is meditating, or he is busy, or he is on a journey, or perhaps he is sleeping and must be awakened." Driven to desperation, the prophets engage in ritual self-mutilation, gashing themselves until the blood flows, but still, "there was no voice; no one answered, no one paid attention."

At evening, Elijah calls the people to him. In a powerful symbolic act, he rebuilds the Lord's altar with twelve stones, representing the twelve tribes of a divided Israel. He digs a trench around it, prepares the bull, and then, to eliminate any possibility of trickery, orders the entire assembly to douse the sacrifice and the wood with water three times, until the trench itself is filled. Elijah offers a simple prayer, and immediately, the fire of the Lord falls. It consumes the burnt sacrifice, the wood, the stones, the dust, and even licks up all the water in the trench. The people fall on their faces in awe and declare, "The Lord, He is God! The Lord, He is God!" On Elijah's command, the people seize the 450 prophets of Baal and execute them at the Brook Kishon, delivering a devastating blow to Jezebel's religious infrastructure.

When Ahab reports these events to Jezebel in Jezreel, her response is swift and venomous. Unrepentant and enraged by the slaughter of her prophets, she doesn't merely get angry; she sends a messenger to Elijah with a chillingly specific death threat: "So let the gods do to me, and more also, if I do not make your life as the life of one of them by tomorrow about this time." This threat so terrifies Elijah that he flees for his life into the wilderness.

Jezebel recedes from the narrative for a time, but reemerges in 1 Kings 21 to demonstrate that her capacity for evil is undiminished. Her husband, Ahab, covets a nearby vineyard belonging to a righteous man named Naboth, who refuses to sell his ancestral inheritance. When Ahab petulantly sulks in his bed, Jezebel chastises his weakness and seizes control of the situation. She chillingly says, "Are you not the king over Israel? Arise, eat food, and let your heart be cheerful; I will give you the vineyard of Naboth the Jezreelite."

Using Ahab's official signet ring to authenticate letters in his name, she orchestrates a judicial murder. She commands the elders of Jezreel to proclaim a fast, publicly accuse Naboth of blasphemy against God and the king using two hired false witnesses, and then stone him to death. The plan is executed perfectly, and the innocent Naboth is murdered for his property. This act of royal corruption and violence, masterminded by Jezebel, prompts Elijah to return with a final, grim prophecy from God: "In the place where dogs licked the blood of Naboth, dogs shall lick your blood." For Jezebel, he prophesies an even more gruesome fate: "The dogs shall eat Jezebel by the wall of Jezreel."

This prophecy is fulfilled years later in 2 Kings 9. Jehu, a military commander anointed by a successor of Elijah to be king and to cleanse the house of Ahab, rides furiously to Jezreel. Hearing of his approach, the aged Queen Jezebel, ever defiant and regal, does not cower. She prepares for her end with calculated theatrics: she "put paint on her eyes and adorned her head," presenting herself as the powerful queen one last time. Looking down from a window, she greets Jehu not with a plea, but with a searing insult, comparing him to "Zimri," a previous usurper who was also a murderer of his king.

Jehu's response is brutal and decisive. He looks up to the window and shouts, "Who is on my side? Who?" Two or three eunuchs—her own court officials—peer down. On Jehu's order, they throw her from the window. Her body is trampled by Jehu's horse and chariot below. Jehu then casually enters the palace to eat and drink, later commanding his servants to retrieve the body of "this cursed woman" for burial. They found only her skull, her feet, and the palms of her hands; the dogs had devoured the rest, exactly as the word of the Lord through Elijah had declared.

Yet, Jezebel's sinister legacy did not die with her. Her daughter, Athaliah, who had been married into the royal line of Judah, upon hearing of her son's death, seized the throne in Jerusalem and executed all her royal rivals to become the only queen to reign over Judah. The biblical account judges her as even more evil than her mother, demonstrating how the toxic influence of Jezebel—of idolatry, ruthless power, and violence—continued to plague the nations of Israel and Judah long after her gruesome death.

*****

As we conclude our exploration of 2 Kings, we encounter a profoundly moving narrative that introduces us to the sixth and final barren woman of the Old Testament. Though her name is lost to history, her story, found in 2 Kings 4:8-37, is one of the most powerful accounts of faith, tragedy, and miraculous redemption in the scriptures.

She is identified only as the Shunammite woman, a resident of the town of Shunem, which lay on a prominent route frequented by the prophet Elisha. This woman was not only wealthy but also remarkably kind and righteous. Recognizing Elisha as a holy man of God, she and her elderly husband began to extend their hospitality to him, insisting he dine with them whenever he passed through. Her devotion grew to such an extent that she conceived a beautiful gesture of pious generosity: she and her husband built a private, furnished upper room on their roof, a dedicated sanctuary for Elisha. This small chamber was equipped with a bed, a table, a chair, and a lampstand, ensuring the prophet had a place of rest and solitude.

Deeply touched by this extraordinary kindness, Elisha felt compelled to repay her. He summoned her and offered to speak to the king or the commander of the army on her behalf, an offer of immense political influence. But the Shunammite woman, content in her life and community, gracefully declined, stating, "I dwell among my own people." Her motives were purely selfless; she sought no earthly reward for her faithfulness.

Unsatisfied and determined to bless her, Elisha turned to his servant, Gehazi, for insight. Gehazi observed, "She has no son, and her husband is old." Understanding this as the deepest, unspoken longing of her heart, Elisha summoned her again. As she stood in the doorway, he made an incredible prophecy: "At this season, about this time next year, you shall embrace a son."

Her reaction was not one of immediate joy but of stunned disbelief and a plea born from a lifetime of resigned sorrow. "No, my lord, O man of God; do not lie to your servant," she begged, fearing the cruel pain of a hope raised only to be dashed.

Yet, the word of the prophet was true. She conceived and bore a son at the very time Elisha had promised. The impossible had happened; her home, once quiet, was now filled with the joy of a child.

Years passed, and the boy grew. Then, a devastating tragedy struck. While out in the field with his father during the harvest, the young boy suddenly cried out, "My head, my head!" He was carried to his mother and died in her lap at noon that very day.

In her profound and desperate grief, the Shunammite woman exhibited astonishing resolve. Rather than surrendering to despair, she acted with unwavering faith. She carried her son's body up to the prophet's chamber, laid him on Elisha's bed, and shut the door. Without telling her husband the full truth—saying only, "It will be well"—she urgently commanded a servant to saddle a donkey so she could go to the man of God.

She raced to Mount Carmel, where Elisha was staying. Seeing her approaching with such fierce determination, Elisha sent Gehazi out to greet her. When Gehazi asked if all was well, she offered a cryptic, faith-filled reply: "It is well." But upon reaching Elisha himself, she fell at his feet, grasping them in a posture of utter desperation. Gehazi moved to push her away, but Elisha stopped him, perceiving the deep anguish she hid from everyone else. "Your servant has no pain," she finally confessed, her words heavy with a meaning only Elisha could understand. She was not there for comfort, but for a miracle.

Elisha immediately dispatched Gehazi ahead with his staff, instructing him to lay it on the boy's face. But the Shunammite woman refused to leave without Elisha himself, declaring, "As the LORD lives, and as you yourself live, I will not leave you." So Elisha rose and followed her.

Gehazi arrived first and placed the staff on the boy's face, but there was no sound or movement. The power was not in the object, but in the prophet. When Elisha arrived, he entered the upper room alone and shut the door. He prayed fervently to the LORD. Then, in an intimate and physical act, he stretched himself upon the boy’s body, mouth to mouth, eyes to eyes, hands to hands. As he did, the child's body grew warm. Elisha got up, paced the room, and then stretched himself over the boy a second time. This time, the boy sneezed seven times and opened his eyes.

Elisha called the Shunammite woman, and as she entered, he presented her with her living son. She fell at his feet, bowing to the ground in overwhelmed gratitude, before taking her resurrected child into her arms. Her faith, her persistence, and her righteous generosity had been met with the ultimate blessing: life from death, the definitive proof of God's power working through his prophet.

The Hidden Queen: Esther

The story of Queen Esther stands as one of the most riveting and enduring narratives within the Old Testament, holding a place of honor alongside foundational tales like the Exodus during Passover and the legendary duel of David and Goliath. Unlike many biblical figures who were prophets or warriors, Esther's heroism is one of cunning, courage, and strategic diplomacy, playing out within the opulent and perilous confines of a Persian palace. Her story is a masterful blend of political thriller, romantic tension, and divine providence, though notably, God is never explicitly mentioned in the entire text.

This timeless tale of a young Jewish woman who risked her life to save her people from genocide has captivated audiences for millennia. Its dramatic potential has made it a frequent subject for adaptation, inspiring numerous Hollywood films, from the classic 1948 silent film The Feast of Esther to more modern interpretations, as well as countless novels, plays, and works of art. A single, powerful line from the Book of Esther has even transcended its religious origins to become a mainstay in pop culture, often used to inspire a sense of destiny and purpose. The original verse (Esther 4:14) questions, "And who knows whether you have come to the kingdom for such a time as this?" Though it is almost universally misquoted and softened into the more declarative, "You were chosen for such a time as this," the sentiment resonates deeply, offering a message of empowerment and timely responsibility.

Esther's legacy is so profound that it is cemented into the very rhythm of Jewish life through the joyous and raucous holiday of Purim. This festival commemorates the victory of the Jews over their oppressor, Haman, and is celebrated with festive meals, gift-giving, charity, and the public reading of the Megillah (the Scroll of Esther). During the reading, congregations erupt in noise with groggers (noisemakers) and stomping feet to drown out the name of the villain Haman, truly bringing the ancient story to life in a vibrant, communal celebration.

So, let us prepare to delve into the extraordinary life of this "Hidden Queen"—a woman who concealed her identity until a critical moment, whose story remains unique in the biblical canon, and whose courage continues to inspire the assertion that a single individual, heeding the call of destiny, can alter the course of history.

*****

The Book of Esther opens not with its titular heroine, but with a powerful and assertive woman whose brief, defiant stand sets the entire plot in motion: Queen Vashti. Her story, though occupying only a single chapter, is crucially important to Esther's narrative, establishing the high-stakes, patriarchal political climate in which Esther must later operate.

The narrative begins by grounding itself in specific historical and geographical context. We are introduced to the opulent court of King Ahasuerus (historically identified as Xerxes I), who rules over a vast empire stretching from India to Ethiopia, the Persian-Median powerhouse that constitutes much of modern-day Iran. His throne is situated in the magnificent capital city of Shushan (Susa), within the fortified citadel that served as the administrative heart of his domain.

The catalyst for the story is the king's extravagant display of wealth and power. After a marathon 180-day exhibition designed to awe and intimidate the princes, nobles, and military leaders of his 127 provinces, Ahasuerus caps the festivities with a lavish, week-long feast for all the men of the citadel. The description of the event emphasizes sheer opulence: courtyards adorned with fine linen and marble, couches of gold and silver, and an abundance of royal wine served in golden vessels. Simultaneously, Queen Vashti hosts a separate, parallel feast for the women of the royal court, a detail that underscores the segregated social norms of the time.

The crisis erupts on the seventh and final day. The king, "merry with wine" and intoxicated by his own power and indulgence, decides to make Queen Vashti the culminating spectacle of his feast. He commands his seven designated eunuchs to summon the queen. His specific order is that she appear before the assembled drunken nobility wearing her royal crown. The implication, debated by scholars, is that he may have wanted her to wear only her crown—to parade her beauty as his ultimate possession before his leering guests.

Vashti's response is stunning and unprecedented. She flatly refuses the king's command. This is not merely the act of a modest woman; it is a public, political act of defiance from a queen who asserts her own autonomy and refuses to be objectified. Her refusal throws the court into chaos. The king's rage is incendiary, but it is also impotent. In his fury, he turns not to force, but to protocol, consulting his circle of seven wise men and legal experts "who knew the times"—the customs and laws of the Persians and Medes.

The advisors, led by Memucan, frame Vashti's personal disobedience as a national crisis with terrifying implications for the social order. Their reasoning reveals the profound fragility of the patriarchal system: "Vashti the queen has not only wronged the king, but also all the princes, and all the people who are in all the provinces of King Ahasuerus. For the queen's behavior will become known to all women, causing them to look with contempt on their husbands... There will be excessive contempt and wrath."

Their proposed solution is therefore not a private admonishment but a drastic, empire-wide decree. They advise the king to permanently depose Vashti and give her royal position to "another who is better than she." This decree, to be proclaimed in every province and in every language, would explicitly state that every man should be the ruler of his own household. This move is a blatant piece of political theater designed to use the law to crush a nascent movement of female independence before it can begin, using Vashti as a brutal example to "keep all the women in their place."

King Ahasuerus, perhaps seeing the political wisdom in their fear-based counsel, agrees. Letters are dispatched throughout the empire, and Queen Vashti is irrevocably dethroned. This opening episode provides a startling glimpse into the second-class status of women in the ancient court, where a queen's autonomy could be legally annulled to serve the king's wounded pride and maintain systemic control. It is into this vacuum of power, created by one woman's courageous and costly stand for dignity, that the young Esther will soon step, foreshadowing that the conflict between male authority and female agency is far from over.

*****

Following the dramatic deposition of Queen Vashti for her defiance, King Ahasuerus's rage subsided into regret. His court officials, the wise men and princes of Persia, grew concerned for the king's solemn mood and the stability of the royal household. Seeking a solution, they proposed a meticulously organized search throughout the empire's 127 provinces for a new queen. This was not merely a suggestion but a royal decree: all beautiful young virgins were to be gathered into the citadel of Susa and placed under the care of Hegai, the king's eunuch and custodian of the women. There, they would undergo a mandatory twelve-month beautification regimen—six months with oil of myrrh and six with perfumes and cosmetics—in preparation for their individual audience with the king. This imperial beauty contest was designed to find a woman who would not only please the king visually but, they hoped, would also prove more compliant than her predecessor.

It is at this juncture that the narrative shifts to introduce a key figure: Mordecai, a Jew from the tribe of Benjamin, whose family had been exiled from Jerusalem during the Babylonian captivity. He was a legal guardian and much older cousin to a young woman named Hadassah, which means "myrtle" in Hebrew, symbolizing righteousness.

Following the death of her parents, Mordecai had adopted her as his own daughter, raising her with deep affection and wisdom. The text poignantly notes that Hadassah, whom we come to know by her Persian name, Esther ("star"), was "lovely and beautiful," a detail that underscores her outward qualification for the king's decree, though her true beauty was rooted in her character.

When the king's command was issued, Esther, like so many other young women, was forcibly taken from her home and brought to the king's harem. Though this was a terrifying and involuntary upheaval, the unseen hand of divine providence was already at work. Upon her arrival, Esther immediately found favor in the eyes of Hegai, the chief eunuch. Recognizing something special in her—perhaps her humility, grace, or demeanor—Hegai accelerated her preparation. He provided her with extra portions of the coveted beauty treatments beyond her standard allowance, selected seven choice maidservants from the king's palace to attend her, and swiftly moved her and her attendants to the best apartments within the harem. This preferential treatment, occurring despite Esther's status as a foreign captive, signals a guiding providence shaping events for a purpose not yet revealed.

A critical layer of the story is established here: secrecy. Mordecai had sternly instructed Esther not to reveal her ethnic identity or her Jewish family background. Scholars posit that Mordecai himself may have given her the Persian name Esther to help conceal her Hebrew origins, a prudent precaution for a minority people living in exile. This theme of remaining "hidden" becomes a central thread in the narrative, suggesting that timing and discernment are crucial. Even from afar, Mordecai's paternal concern was relentless. He paced back and forth every day in front of the court of the women's quarters, anxiously seeking any news about Esther's welfare and what was happening to her, a powerful image of his deep love and protectiveness.

After the full twelve months of prescribed preparation, each young woman was granted one night to go in to the king. The ritual was elaborate and final. Each could request whatever jewelry or adornment she desired from the harem to present herself before the monarch. However, the stakes were profoundly high. If the king was not pleased, she would not return to the virgins' quarters but would be relegated to the secondary harem of concubines, under the care of Shaashgaz, another eunuch, likely never to see the king again.

When Esther's turn finally arrived, she demonstrated remarkable wisdom and humility. Contrary to others who may have laden themselves with finery, she requested nothing but what Hegai, who knew the king's tastes intimately, advised her to take. Her trust in his guidance proved decisive. She found immense favor in the king's eyes—more than any other woman—and he loved her. Placing the royal crown upon her head, Ahasuerus proclaimed Esther the new queen in Vashti's place and held a great feast in her honor, "Esther's feast," proclaiming a holiday throughout the provinces and distributing gifts with royal generosity.

Despite her new exalted status, Esther remained obedient to Mordecai's initial command, continuing to keep her Jewish heritage a secret. Her loyalty to her cousin-father also remained unwavering. This fidelity soon had a decisive impact on the king's own security. Mordecai, now sitting at the king's gate—a position indicating some level of official status—overheard a plot by two of the king's chamberlains, Bigthan and Teresh, to assassinate Ahasuerus. He immediately relayed the vital information to Queen Esther, who reported it to the king, prudently giving credit to Mordecai. An investigation confirmed the conspiracy, the two eunuchs were hanged, and the event was recorded in the royal chronicles in Mordecai's name, a seemingly minor detail that would later prove to be of monumental importance. This chain of events illustrates how the faithful actions of the hidden ones, Esther and Mordecai, were quietly positioning them to become instruments of salvation.

*****

The narrative of Esther takes a dark and pivotal turn in its third chapter with the introduction of its true antagonist: Haman. This is not merely a rival official, but a man whose pride and wounded ego would set in motion a genocidal plot. Identified with contemptuous specificity as "Haman the son of Hammedatha, the Agagite," his lineage is a critical detail. The Agagites were descendants of Agag, the king of the Amalekites—a nation perpetually at odds with Israel, representing an ancient and bitter enmity ordained for destruction. This established him not just as a personal foe to Mordecai, but as a hereditary enemy of the entire Jewish people.

His entry into the story is one of exalted power. King Ahasuerus, whose whimsical and distant governance creates a power vacuum, elevates Haman above all the other princes and nobles of the vast Persian empire. The king commands that all royal servants at the gate bow down and pay homage to this new vizier, a gesture acknowledging his unparalleled authority. For a time, the court obeys—all except one man: Mordecai the Jew. His refusal is not a sudden, hot-headed act of rebellion, but a quiet, steadfast daily defiance. When the other officials at the king's gate, perplexed and alarmed by this insubordination, press him for an explanation, Mordecai reveals his core identity, telling them he is a Jew, implying a fundamental religious and ethnic conviction that forbade him from offering such reverence to a man.

These courtiers, perhaps seeking favor or merely concerned with maintaining order, carry this troubling news to Haman. They do not merely report the act of disobedience; they specifically emphasize Mordecai's Jewishness, subtly framing it as the root cause. This revelation ignites a fire in Haman. However, his anger transcends mere irritation at a single subordinate's insolence. To learn that Mordecai was a Jew connected the personal slight to his deep-seated ancestral hatred. The text suggests that Haman initially "disdained to lay hands on Mordecai alone," a phrase hinting at a calculated fear. A man of such immense pride would crave a personal and humiliating revenge, but the knowledge of Mordecai's people—a distinct, cohesive, and widespread community within the empire—gave him pause. To attack one Jew might provoke a reaction from all. His pride demanded a retaliation so vast and absolute that retaliation would be impossible.

Thus, Haman's malice curdles into a monstrous solution. He would not settle for punishing a single man; he would eradicate the entire nation from which Mordecai came. In a chilling audience with King Ahasuerus, Haman cleverly disguises his vendetta as a matter of state security. He portrays the Jewish people as a scattered, alien nation within the empire's provinces, a people whose laws are "different from those of every other people," and who do not keep the king's laws. He insinuates they are a seditious element, implying it is not in the king's best interest to tolerate them. With breathtaking cynicism, he then offers to personally finance the entire genocide, transferring ten thousand talents of silver into the royal treasury to pay for the slaughter, a move designed to make the decree appear selfless and to guarantee the avaricious king's cooperation.

The tragically disengaged Ahasuerus, seemingly without a second thought or a single question, agrees. He gives Haman his signet ring—the ultimate symbol of his authority—effectively granting him carte blanche to write the decree in the king's own name. Letters are then drafted and sent by couriers to every single province of the empire, from India to Ethiopia, written in each local language. The decree gave a single, horrifying instructions: on a specific day, the thirteenth day of the twelfth month, the people of every province were to arm themselves and "destroy, to kill, and to annihilate all Jews, young and old, women and children, in one day." The scope of evil is terrifying in its completeness.

It is at this moment of profound darkness that the purpose of Esther's seemingly fortuitous ascension to queen becomes terrifyingly clear. Her royal position was never merely a reward for her beauty or a romantic subplot; it was divine positioning. Placed in the very heart of the Persian power structure, she alone possessed the potential access and influence to intercede on behalf of her people against an enemy who had just been given the full, irrevocable authority of the king himself. The stakes could not be higher.

*****

The dreadful news of Haman's genocidal decree did not merely arrive; it erupted like a seismic shock through the Jewish diaspora in the vast Persian Empire. A cold wave of terror and disbelief washed over the people, followed by the paralyzing heat of despair. The official proclamation, stamped with the king's own signet ring, was not a vague threat but a death sentence, authorizing their utter annihilation on a single, predetermined day.

In the capital of Shushan, the horror found its most profound expression in Mordecai. Upon hearing the decree, his reaction was immediate and visceral—a public performance of ultimate grief. He tore his fine garments, rending them from his body as an outward symbol of a heart torn apart. He cast aside all dignity, clothing himself in the rough, abrasive texture of sackcloth—a garment of slaves and mourners—and covered his head in a mantle of coarse ashes. Wailing loudly, he moved through the city, not to his own home, but straight into the heart of the public square, stopping at the king's gate, a place where he could neither enter in his wretched state nor be ignored. His was not a private sorrow but a national lamentation made flesh. His agonized cries were a siren, and soon, they echoed throughout every province. From the greatest to the least, the Jewish people followed his lead, donning sackcloth, fasting, weeping, and lying in ashes, engulfed by a collective mourning for a future that had been stolen.

Within the insulated luxury of the royal harem, Queen Esther remained initially unaware of the cataclysm unfolding beyond her gilded walls. The news reached her indirectly, as her maids and eunuchs, their faces pale with anxiety, whispered of her cousin Mordecai's shocking and public display of anguish. Disturbed and deeply troubled by the image of her steadfast guardian brought so low, Esther's first instinct was one of comfort and remedy. She urgently dispatched a set of fresh, dignified robes to Mordecai, a practical and compassionate attempt to clothe him in honor again and lift him from the dust. But the gesture was returned. Mordecai refused the garments outright. His mourning was not for a personal loss that could be soothed; it was for an existential threat that demanded action.

Realizing the gravity of the situation was far beyond a simple misfortune, Esther turned to a trusted intermediary, Hathach, one of the king's eunuchs specifically assigned to attend to her. She commanded him to go to Mordecai and to discover the precise cause of this profound despair. Hathach obeyed, finding the mourner at the king's gate, a figure of dust and grief amidst the polished marble and gold. There, Mordecai unburdened himself completely. He told Hathach everything: the vindictive pride of Haman, the malicious edict, the promised plunder, and the appointed day of slaughter. To ensure Esther understood this was no rumor, he provided Hathach with a physical copy of the decree itself—the cold, bureaucratic language sanctioning murder.

But Mordecai gave Hathach more than information; he gave him a mission. He instructed the eunuch to relay every detail to Esther and to lay upon her a solemn charge: she must go boldly into the inner court to King Ahasuerus. She was to make supplication before him, to plead for the life of her people, and to intercede for their deliverance. The fate of every Jew now rested on her shoulders.

When Hathach delivered this terrifying directive, Esther's response was not one of refusal but of stark, fearful reality. She sent a message back to Mordecai, explaining the immutable law of the palace: that any person, man or woman, who approached the king in the inner court without an explicit summons was condemned to death. The only exception was if the king himself extended his golden scepter, a gesture of clemency that was entirely at his whim. And she added, with chilling emphasis, that this law applied even to her, the queen. Her privileged position was a gilded cage, not a shield.

Hathach carried this desperate reply to Mordecai, who received it not as an excuse, but as a challenge to Esther's faith. His answer to her was the now-famous, pivotal speech that would change history. He dismissed her fear of the palace's law with a dose of terrifying truth: "Do not imagine that you, of all the Jews, will escape with your life just because you are in the king's palace. If you persist in staying silent at this critical time, relief and deliverance for the Jews will inevitably come from some other place—for God will not abandon His people. But you and your entire family will perish. And who knows?" he concluded, his message cutting to the very heart of her destiny. "Perhaps you have attained your royal position precisely for such a time as this."

His words were a spark in the dark, transforming her fear into resolve. Esther's next message to Mordecai showed a complete transformation. No longer a frightened girl, she spoke as a queen and a leader. She issued a command: He was to gather all the Jews living in Shushan and lead them in a solemn, absolute fast on her behalf. For three days and three nights, they were to eat no food and drink no water. This was not a diet but a desperate spiritual siege, an appeal for divine favor to accompany her mortal courage. And she vowed to join them in this sacred act of devotion, declaring that she and her maids would do the same. "Then," she said, "I will go to the king, even though it is against the law. And if I perish, I perish."

Mordecai did not hesitate. He went out and did all that Esther had commanded him, mobilizing the community in a unified front of prayer and supplication. For three days, a holy silence of anticipation fell over the Jews of Shushan, their empty stomachs a testament to their full hearts, their hopes pinned on the courage of one woman prepared to risk everything.

*****

After three days and nights of solemn prayer and fasting, a period in which she had abstained from all food and drink to seek divine favor, Esther felt a fragile resolve harden within her. Dismissing the plain garments of her supplication, she clothed herself in the magnificent regalia of her office. The weight of the crown upon her brow was nothing compared to the weight of an entire people upon her shoulders. With a final, steadying breath, she stepped from her chambers to approach the king's inner court, a place where her very presence could mean instant death.

As she crossed the threshold into the dazzling, gold-adorned hall, all eyes turned to her. King Ahasuerus, ensconced upon his throne, looked up. For a heart-stopping moment, his expression was unreadable. Then, his countenance softened, and love for his queen overrode the stern law of the Persians. He extended the golden scepter, the symbol of life and mercy. Trembling, Esther stepped forward and touched its tip, her relief a palpable force in the room. The king's voice, filled with warmth and concern, broke the silence: "What troubles you, Queen Esther? What is your request? Even to half of my kingdom, it shall be granted to you."

Yet, courage, once mustered, now demanded strategy. Rather than revealing her grave purpose in the public court, she invited the king and his highest noble, the villainous Haman, to a private banquet she had prepared. The king, delighted, immediately agreed and summoned Haman, who swelled with pride at the exclusive invitation.

At the intimate feast, amid the fragrance of wine and fine foods, the king posed his generous question again: "What is your petition, Queen Esther? It shall be granted you. What is your request? Up to half the kingdom, it shall be performed!" Once more, Esther deferred, asking only that they both return for another banquet the following day. Puzzled but enamored, the king consented.

Meanwhile, Haman's euphoria was short-lived. Leaving the palace, he again encountered Mordecai, the Jew who refused to pay him any homage. The familiar rage boiled within him, but he choked it down, returning to his home to gather his wife, Zeresh, and all his friends. There, he boasted of his immense wealth, his multitude of children, and the singular honor of being the only courtier invited to Queen Esther's banquets. "Yet," he lamented, "all this is worth nothing to me every time I see that Jew Mordecai sitting at the king's gate." Seizing on his hubris, Zeresh and his friends proposed a brutal solution: "Let a gallows be made, seventy-five feet high, and in the morning suggest to the king that Mordecai be hanged on it. Then you can go merrily with the king to the banquet." The idea delighted Haman, and he ordered the monstrous structure built immediately.

That very night, divine providence intervened. King Ahasuerus could not sleep. To pass the hours, he ordered the book of chronicles—the official record of his reign—to be brought and read aloud. The servant, perhaps guided by an unseen hand, read the account of how Mordecai had once uncovered the assassination plot of Bigthana and Teresh, saving the king's life. Ahasuerus, struck by the memory, asked, "What honor or dignity has been bestowed on Mordecai for this?" His servants replied, "Nothing has been done for him."

At that precise moment, a noise was heard in the outer court. The king inquired, "Who is in the court?" It was Haman, arriving in the pre-dawn hours, his mind filled with the plot to murder Mordecai. Before he could speak his dark request, the king summoned him in and posed a question dripping with tragic irony: "What should be done for the man the king delights to honor?"

Blinded by arrogance, Haman assumed the king spoke of him. He envisioned the highest honor imaginable: "For the man whom the king delights to honor, let a royal robe be brought which the king himself has worn, and a horse the king has ridden, with a royal crest on its head. Let the robes and the horse be entrusted to one of the king's most noble princes, so that he may array the man and lead him on horseback through the city square, proclaiming, 'This is what is done for the man the king delights to honor!'"

The king's response was a devastating blow: "Hurry! Take the robe and the horse, as you have said, and do so for Mordecai the Jew, who sits at the king's gate. Leave out nothing you have suggested." The man who came to secure a death warrant was instead commanded to publicly exalt his most hated enemy. Humiliated, Haman was forced to parade Mordecai through the streets, proclaiming the very words he had dreamed would be for himself. He then rushed home, head covered in shame, to mourn this terrible turn of events. His wise men and his wife, Zeresh, saw the hand of fate in this and delivered a chilling prophecy: "If Mordecai, before whom you have begun to fall, is of Jewish descent, you will not prevail against him but will surely fall before him."

As they spoke, the king's eunuchs arrived, hurriedly escorting a despondent Haman to Queen Esther's second banquet. There, with the wine served, the king for the third time asked for her petition. Now, the time for hesitation was over. Esther's voice was clear and strong as she revealed her truth: "If I have found favor in your sight, O king, and if it pleases the king, let my life be given me at my petition, and my people at my request. For we have been sold, I and my people, to be destroyed, to be killed, and to be annihilated."

The king, aghast and furious, demanded, "Who is he, and where is he, who would dare to do such a thing?" Esther pointed directly at the horrified courtier and declared, "The adversary and enemy is this vile Haman!" At that moment, Haman's world collapsed. Terrified, he saw the wrath on the king's face. Ahasuerus stormed out into the palace garden to master his rage. Desperate, Haman remained behind, falling upon the couch where Queen Esther was reclining to beg for his life. As the king returned, he misinterpreted the scene, seeing not a supplicant but an assailant threatening his queen. A guard instantly covered Haman's face, a sign of condemnation.

One of the eunuchs noted the towering gallows Haman had built at his house for Mordecai. The king's order was swift and final: "Hang him on it!" So, Haman was executed upon the very instrument of death he had constructed for the righteous Mordecai. The king's wrath subsided, and that same day, he gave Haman's estate to Queen Esther, who put Mordecai in charge of it. Mordecai was elevated to the king's service, and Esther pleaded with the king to revoke the genocidal edict. While a decree of the Medes and Persians could not be undone, the king empowered Esther and Mordecai to write a new decree, granting the Jews in every city the right to assemble and defend themselves.

When the appointed day arrived, the Jews triumphed over their enemies, but they took no plunder, demonstrating that their fight was for survival, not greed. To commemorate their deliverance from destruction, Esther and Mordecai instituted the feast of Purim—named for the "pur" or lot that Haman had cast to determine the date of their annihilation—a joyous celebration that endures to this day as a testament to courage, providence, and the reversal of fortune.

The Book of Esther Study Guide

Background and Introduction:

Esther belongs to the period after the Babylonian exile, when Persia had replaced Babylon as the ruling power. It is believed to be written by Mordicai. The story is set in Shushan, one of the Persian capitals(Esther's palace still stands in Susa,Iran), during the reign of King Ahasuerus, better known by his Greek name, Xerxes I (486–464 BC). Some Israelites had returned to Jerusalem, where they enjoyed a reasonable amount of control over their own affairs. Others, like Esther and Mordecai, were still in exile. God is not directly mentioned by name in the book of Esther, but it shows clearly that, even when God is most hidden, he is still working to protect his children.
Chronologically, the book of Daniel occurs towards the end of the Babylonian captivity between 605 BC and 530 BC. The book of Esther occurs later, between 486 BC and 465 BC(about 100 years), after many Jews had returned to Jerusalem and rebuilt the temple. The temple restoration was completed in 515 BC and happened between the Daniel and Esther narratives.

Esther's name in Hebrew means star or a bright star, however because Esther is her persian name we must look at the persian pronunciation and meaning,Ishtar(Eash-Shtar) which means hidden. As we go through this book you'll find the hidden theme a lot, and the reason why that is can be found in Deuteronomy 31:16-18.

16 And the Lord said to Moses: "Behold, you will rest with your fathers; and this people will rise and play the harlot with the gods of the foreigners of the land, where they go *to be* among them, and they will forsake Me and break My covenant which I have made with them. **17** Then My anger shall be aroused against them in that day, and I will forsake them, and I will hide My face from them, and they shall be devoured. And many evils and troubles shall befall them, so that they will say in that day, 'Have not these evils come upon us because our God *is* not among us?' **18** And I will surely hide My face in that day because of all the evil which they have done, in that they have turned to other gods.

Earlier I said the name of God didn't appear directly in the book of Esther, but it is hidden 5 times throughout the book The Name of YHWH appears encoded in the Hebrew text of Esther through what is called NOTARIKON.
A Notarikon is an acronym; anagram or acrostic. Taking the first or last letters of the words of a phrase and joining them to make a new word or, conversely, expanding a word into a phrase, and we will cover those as we get to them. We covered Esther's name and God's promise in Deuteronomy and there is another name (Mordecai) dealing with hiding that we will go over as well.

CHAPTER 1

1:2 Shushan, Persia is modern day Susa, Iran(Esther's Palace aka the Palace of Susa is still there) Ahasuerus is Xerxes I

1:20 All wives will honor their husbands both great and small.

HWHY

4 3 2 1

הִיא וְכָל־ הַנָּשִׁים יִתְּנוּ

1 2 3 4

Hi' W^{e}kal Hannashim Yitt^{e}nu.

1 2 3 4

it and-all the-wives shall-give

CHAPTER 2

2:5 We are introduced to Mordecai, whose name has a double or hidden meaning. In the Persian tongue Mordukai which means Servant of Morduk. Morduk is a chief Persian god. In the Hebrew tongue it is Mordecayah which means servant of YHWH. He is a Benjamite descended from Jacob's youngest son Benjamin

2:6 This means Mordecai and Esther's Ancestors were captured in Jerusalem and then carried to Babylon with Daniel.

2:7 Here we meet Hadassah (Esther's real name) which means Myrtle. The myrtle tree in the Bible represents beauty, abundance, blessings, prosperity, restoration, and God's faithfulness. She is Mordecai's younger cousin and as mentioned in verse 5 along with Mordecai she is a Benjamite making them both distant ancestors to the Apostle Paul(Romans 11:1 and Philippians 3:5)who is also a Benjamite.

2:10 again the Hidden theme in this book

CHAPTER 3

3:8 The laws Hamen are referring to here are the levitical laws found mostly in Exodus,Leviticus and Deuteronomy

3:12 Satraps are a unique position in the Persian Empire, they were like governors but had unique responsibilities like collecting taxes

CHAPTER 4

Chapter 4 is one big back and forth message passing between Mordecai and Esther

CHAPTER 5

5:4 second hidden name of YHWH

4 3 2 1

הַיּוֹם וְהָמָן הַמֶּלֶךְ יָבוֹא

1 2 3 4

Yabo' Hammelek W^eHaman Hayyom

1 2 3 4

let-come the-king and-Haman this-day

5:13 Third hidden name of YHWH

4 3 2 1

לִי שֹׁוֶה אֵינֶנּוּ זֶה

1 2 3 4

zeH 'eynennW shoveH l^{e}*Y*

1 3 2 4

this availeth nothing to-me

5:14 a cubit is 18 inches so we are talking about a 75 foot tall gallows.

CHAPTER 6

6:7 Haman unintentionally rewards the man he was out to execute by way of the funniest case of mistaken identity ever written.

CHAPTER 7

7:5 The 4th hidden name of YHWH

4 3 2 1

זֶה וְאֵי זֶה הוּא

1 2 3 4

*hu'**E** ze**H** v*$^{e'}$*e**Y** ze**H***

1 2 3 4

[who is] he this [man] and where [is] this [man]

EHYH is Ehyah (E-Hey-YaH) simply means I AM

The only time it is used in scripture is in Exodus 3:14
And God said to Moses, "I AM WHO I AM." And He said, "Thus you shall say to the children of Israel, 'I AM has sent me to you.' "

And God said to Moses, "EHYAH ASHER EHYAH." And He said, "Thus you shall say to the children of Israel, 'EHYAH has sent me to you.' "

EHYAH ASHER EHYAH means I AM WHO IS AND WILL REMAIN I AM

7:7 The 5th and final hidden name of YHWH

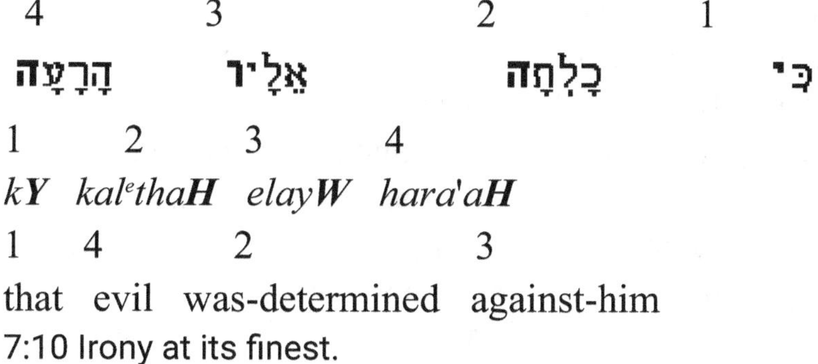

4 3 2 1

הָרָעָה אֵלָיו כָלְתָה כִּי

1 2 3 4

kY kal^{e}thaH elayW hara'aH

1 4 2 3

that evil was-determined against-him

7:10 Irony at its finest.

CHAPTER 8

8:1 Esther is given Hamen's house and then comes clean to the King about Mordecai.

8:2 Mordecai is elevated to Hamen's old position and Esther gives him Haman's house.

8:5 Esther is talking about the decrees from chapter 3 that are still in effect.

8:8 King Ahasuerus gave Esther and Mordecai power of attorney to reverse the letters.

8:11 The Israelites were given the right to bear arms and protect themselves by any means necessary.

8:15 Notice Mordecai's robes are blue and white, the same colors as the levitical priest tzitzits(braided cords worn on the waist or belt line). This is because Blue represents divinity and white represents Holiness and purity.

CHAPTER 9

9:18 This is where the Feast of Purim comes from. Purim is celebrated to honor and remember what Queen Esther did for the Jewish people. It is the only feast not appointed by YHWH, but still fun to celebrate because the kids get to dress up as people from the story and put on a play and there is a huge feast to partake in along with music,dancing and scripture reading. Purim this year starts on Thursday March 13 at sundown and ends on Friday March 14 at sundown.

9:20 Mordecai establishes Purim

9:26 This is how we got the name Purim

9:29 Queen Esther endorses Purim

CHAPTER 10

This whole chapter confirms Mordecai's advancement in the kingdom.

Old Testament Conclusion

Our journey through the tapestry of women in the Old Testament has been a profound exploration of faith, power, and humanity. We have stood with the formidable matriarchs of Israel—Sarah, Rebekah, Leah, and Rachel—whose lives, though fraught with struggle, laid the very foundation of a nation chosen by God. We witnessed the breathtaking bravery of Jochebed, who, facing an unimaginable threat, devised a plan that not only saved her son Moses but placed him in the house of Pharaoh, setting the stage for the great Exodus.

We have been inspired by the steadfast righteousness of Hannah, a woman whose deep sorrow was met with fervent prayer. Her faith was rewarded not just with a son, but with the prophet Samuel, the greatest judge Israel would ever know, who would anoint its first kings. We learned of unwavering love and devotion from Ruth, the Moabite widow whose loyalty to her mother-in-law, Naomi, led her to a foreign land and into the lineage of kings, demonstrating that God's redemptive plan extends beyond all borders. And we marveled at the cunning leadership of Deborah, a prophetess and judge who, from beneath her palm tree, commanded armies and delivered Israel from oppression with strategic brilliance.

From the courts of power, we studied the complex legacies of great queens. We saw Bathsheba, whose story began in tragedy and scandal, yet who, through wisdom and maternal influence, ensured the throne passed to her son Solomon, the wisest of kings. We beheld the courage of Esther, who risked her very life to leverage her position as queen and save her entire people from genocide. And we recoiled at the manipulative and idolatrous reign of Jezebel, the Phoenician princess who became the archetype of the evil queen, whose name is synonymous with treachery and a defiance of God.

But before we close this sacred book and end our journey through the Old Testament, it is vital that we pause to honor those women who otherwise go unseen. We must pay tribute to those who have no detailed stories told of their courage or their failings, who are often merely listed as names—if their names are remembered at all. These women were the silent conduits of history, the wombs through which the promise of a Messiah was carried, generation after generation. Their mention, however brief, is a testament to their indispensable role in the divine narrative.

This honorable list begins in the generation after Solomon, following our study of one of his wives, Queen Naamah, mother of King Rehoboam.

Maacah was not only the mother of King Abijam but also the powerful grandmother of the reformer King Asa, whom she may have influenced before he removed her for her idolatry.

Azubah, whose name means "Forsaken," was the faithful mother of the good King Jehoshaphat, who ushered in an era of peace and prosperity.

The name of Jehoram's mother is lost to history, a silent figure standing beside a king who walked in the ways of the wicked kings of Israel.

Athaliah, a daughter of Jezebel, embodied her mother's ruthlessness. As the mother of King Ahaziah, she later seized the throne herself and nearly ended the Davidic line in a bloody purge.

From the town of Beersheba came Zibiah, the mother of King Joash, who was saved from Athaliah's massacre and raised to restore justice and repair the Temple.

Jecoliah of Jerusalem was the mother of the long-reigning and initially prosperous King Uzziah (also known as Azariah).

Jerusha bore King Jotham, a righteous man who continued his father's work, while the name of Ahaz's mother remains unknown, her story overshadowed by her son's profound wickedness.

Abi (also called Abijah) was the daughter of a priest and the mother of one of Judah's greatest kings, Hezekiah, a man renowned for his passionate reforms and unwavering trust in God during siege and illness.

Hephzibah, whose beautiful name means "My Delight is in Her," was the mother of the notorious King Manasseh, whose long reign was marked by terrible evil, though his story ended in repentant grace.

Meshullemeth was the mother of King Amon, who continued his father Manasseh's early evil ways for a brief, dark two years.

Jedidah, meaning "Beloved," bore the great reformer King Josiah, a boy king who rediscovered the Law and sought to return the entire nation to its covenant with God.

Zebidah was the mother of King Jehoiachin, who ruled for a mere three months before being taken captive to Babylon. And finally, Hamutal was the mother of the last king of Judah, Zedekiah, who witnessed the brutal fall of Jerusalem and the destruction of Solomon's Temple.

Then, the devastating deportation to Babylon took place... And in the ensuing exile and return, a profound silence falls. The sacred record, focused on lists of returning men and priests, omits a crucial detail: the names of the mothers go unrecorded. For generations, these women bore children in a foreign land and raised them in the hope of a promised return, their identities and sacrifices absorbed into the collective struggle of the people.

Yet, our honor roll would be incomplete without one final, powerful, and uncomfortable mention: Gomer. Her story is not found in the annals of kings but in the small, deeply personal book of the prophet Hosea. In a breathtaking act of obedience, God commands the righteous Hosea to marry Gomer, a woman known as a prostitute, not as a punishment, but as a living parable. Through his own heartbreak, Hosea learns the divine heartache of God. Gomer's repeated unfaithfulness and rejection of his love mirror Israel's constant rebellion against their covenant God. Yet, in the stunning conclusion, Hosea is commanded to redeem Gomer from slavery and despair, to buy her back and love her unconditionally. This act provides one of the most powerful portraits of God's relentless, grace-filled love in all of scripture: a love that pursues, redeems, and restores even the most wayward of hearts, just as He has done for us.

Section Two: Women of the New Testament.

The four-century span between the final prophecies of Malachi and the opening narratives of the Gospels is often termed the "400 years of silence," a period where the scriptural record falls quiet. Yet, this silence was not an emptiness; it was a crucible of transformation. When the biblical narrative resumes, the world has dramatically changed. The once-proud nation of Judea is no longer sovereign but exists as a fractious client state under the heavy heel of the Roman Empire. Its people, yearning for a promised Messiah to shatter their political chains, live amidst a complex tapestry of Roman law, Hellenistic culture, and fervent religious expectation.

It is into this world of oppression and hope that the New Testament story bursts forth, and remarkably, the indispensable role of women not only continues but evolves in profound ways. Gone are the days of the great matriarchs like Sarah and Rebecca, who founded nations. In their place emerges a new archetype of female agency within the burgeoning movement of Christ. Women now step forward as devoted disciples, as vital financial supporters funding the ministry from their own means, as insightful teachers within house churches, and as sisters bound not by blood, but by a radical, shared faith. They become the first evangelists, the steadfast comforters, and often, the most courageous adherents in the face of peril.

This is not to diminish the sacred and powerful role of motherhood, which finds its ultimate expression in the New Testament. Our study will begin by honoring two of the most pivotal mothers in all of Scripture: Elizabeth, the aged kinswoman whose miracle child prepares the way for the Lord, and Mary of Nazareth, the young virgin whose faithful "yes" altered the course of human history. From these foundational figures, we will journey alongside a diverse tapestry of women. We will witness a desperate mother's faith result in her daughter's liberation from demonic torment, and we will stand in awe as a grieving father's plea leads to a miraculous resurrection that restores a young girl to life.

Furthermore, we will behold a level of bravery that defies comprehension, as these women demonstrate unwavering devotion while facing the most devastating act of violence ever recorded: the brutal crucifixion of the Lord. While the male disciples fled in fear, these women remained, witnessing the agony, attending to the aftermath, and becoming the first to discover the shocking truth of an empty tomb. In the following pages, you will encounter stories that resonate across the millennia. These are narratives woven with threads of relentless love, unshakeable faith, tender devotion, and a strength that emerges not from power, but from profound conviction. Prepare to meet the women who were not merely characters in the greatest story ever told, but whose choices, courage, and loyalty were essential to its very telling.

The Forebearer's Mother: Elizabeth

In the tumultuous era of King Herod's reign over Judea, we are introduced to a beacon of quiet devotion: a righteous couple named Zacharias and Elizabeth. They were both descended from the priestly tribe of Levi, a lineage that imbued their lives with a sacred heritage. But more importantly than their genealogy, they were described as "righteous and blameless," meticulously and lovingly walking in all the commandments and ordinances of the Lord. Their lives were a seamless tapestry of faith and obedience, a testament to their unwavering devotion.

Yet, in the midst of their piety, they carried a profound and private sorrow. Elizabeth was barren. In a culture where children were seen as a divine blessing and a means of carrying on one's legacy, her childlessness was often misinterpreted as a sign of disfavor. For years, she had carried the quiet ache of unfulfilled longing, a hope deferred that had now, with the passing of time, turned into a settled grief, for both were "well advanced in years."

However, as the stories of their ancestors—Sarah, Rebekah, and Hannah—so powerfully attest, human impossibility is merely the canvas upon which God paints His mightiest works. The divine interruption into their story came during Zacharias's priestly service. By a sacred lot, a

once-in-a-lifetime honor, he was chosen to enter the Holy Place of the temple to burn incense while a congregation of worshippers prayed outside.
It was in this hushed, holy moment, amidst the swirling, fragrant smoke of the offering, that the angel Gabriel suddenly appeared, standing to the right of the altar of incense. Zacharias was gripped by a visceral fear, utterly overwhelmed by the celestial presence. But the angel spoke words of comfort: "Do not be afraid, Zacharias, for your prayer has been heard."

The message was breathtaking. Elizabeth would bear him a son, and they were to name him John. This would not be just any child; he would be a source of overwhelming joy and gladness, not only for them but for multitudes who would rejoice at his birth. Then Gabriel unfolded the magnificent destiny of this promised son:

He would be great in the very sight of the Lord, set apart for a Nazirite vow from birth, refraining from wine and strong drink. He would be filled with the Holy Spirit even from his mother's womb, empowered for his divine mission from the very start. His life's purpose would be to turn the hearts of the children of Israel back to their God. And in a stunning proclamation, Gabriel revealed that this boy would walk in the spirit and power of Elijah, the great prophet of old. His mission would be to reconcile generations, "to turn the hearts of the fathers to the children," and to guide the disobedient toward the wisdom of the righteous, ultimately "to make ready a people prepared for the Lord."

Staggered by the announcement, Zacharias's faith, so long steadfast, faltered at the precipice of the miraculous.

Focusing on their advanced age rather than God's omnipotence, he asked for a sign, questioning, "How shall I know this?" In response, the angel identified himself: "I am Gabriel, who stands in the presence of God, and I was sent to speak to you and to bring you this good news." Because Zacharias did not believe the words, he was given a sign—he would be rendered deaf and unable to speak until the day these events came to pass.

Silenced and secluded in a world of quiet contemplation, Zacharias completed his service and returned home. And just as God had ordained, Elizabeth conceived. For five months, she remained in seclusion, a sacred time of reflection and gratitude, marveling, "Thus the Lord has done for me in the days when He looked on me, to take away my reproach among people."

In her sixth month, her relative Mary, who had herself miraculously conceived Jesus by the Holy Spirit, came to visit. Upon Mary's greeting, a profound moment occurred: the baby John, still within Elizabeth's womb, leaped for joy. Elizabeth, immediately filled with the Holy Spirit, recognized the significance of the moment and the supreme identity of the child Mary carried, proclaiming with a loud cry, "Blessed are you among women, and blessed is the fruit of your womb!"

The final act of the miracle unfolded at the child's circumcision. Assuming he would be named after his father, the relatives were astonished when Elizabeth insisted, "No; he shall be called John." Turning to the still-mute Zacharias, they asked for his confirmation. He motioned for a writing tablet and inscribed the definitive words: "His name is John."

In that very instant of faithful obedience, his mouth was opened, his tongue loosed, and he began to speak, pouring forth praises to God. The first words from his lips after months of silence were not of personal relief, but a magnificent hymn of prophecy, now known as the Benedictus, proclaiming the redemption of Israel and the destined role of his son, John, as the prophet of the Most High, who would go before the Lord to prepare His ways.

*****

In the first section of this book, we delved into the poignant and faith-filled narratives of six barren women from the Old Testament. Their stories, marked by longing, societal shame, and ultimate divine intervention, form a powerful testament to God's ability to bring life from emptiness. Elizabeth, the mother of John the Baptist, stands as a righteous successor to this legacy, a New Testament figure whose life echoes the same pattern of patient faith rewarded by a miraculous birth. Yet, among these revered foremothers, her story resonates with a particularly striking and profound parallel to that of Hannah.

Hannah, a woman deeply distressed by her barrenness, was married to Elkanah, a Levite. Her heartfelt, tear-soaked prayers at the tabernacle in Shiloh were so fervent she was mistaken for being drunk. Similarly, Elizabeth, also advanced in years and married to Zechariah, a priest of the line of Abijah, endured her own lifetime of quiet devotion amid the private grief of childlessness. In both cases, God Himself sovereignly intervened to open their wombs, transforming their shame into overwhelming joy and prophetic praise.

The parallels, however, extend far beyond the miracle of their pregnancies. Both women gave birth to sons who were consecrated to God from the womb and who grew to become monumental figures in salvation history. These sons, Samuel and John, would each hold the unique and solemn distinction of being the last of their kind. Samuel served as the final great Judge of Israel, bridging the turbulent period between the rule of the judges and the establishment of the monarchy. John the Baptist was the last and greatest of the Old Testament prophets, serving as the direct forerunner to the Messiah, closing one epoch and heralding the new.

Furthermore, the lives of these two men were inextricably linked to the rise of great kings. Samuel, guided by God, anointed the young shepherd David, ushering in Israel's golden age and establishing the royal line from which the Messiah would come. John, with a voice crying in the wilderness, fulfilled Isaiah's prophecy by preparing the way for the Lord Himself, publicly proclaiming Jesus as the Lamb of God and thus anointing His ministry. Both Samuel and John served God with unwavering dedication and rugged integrity throughout their entire lives, never deviating from their divine calling.

Tragically, a final somber parallel unites their stories: neither man lived to see the king they championed reach their ultimate pinnacle. Samuel died before witnessing the full glory of King David's reign, and John was beheaded by Herod Antipas before seeing Christ’s crucifixion, resurrection, and the establishment of His eternal kingdom.

To all the women who, like Hannah and Elizabeth, walk the difficult path of barrenness—a path often lined with silent sorrow, unanswered questions, and a sense of isolation—this narrative is for you. I pray you find deep and abiding peace, not in the fulfillment of a specific desire, but in the loving and sovereign arms of God, who sees your pain and holds your story. Do not forget that you are part of a sacred lineage. History testifies that by the mighty hand of God, the most profound greatness has often sprouted from wombs once deemed barren. Your value and purpose are not defined by your fruitfulness, but by your faith, and God's plans for you are still brimming with hope and potential.

The Blessed Mother: Mary

When you hear the resonant and singular phrase, “Blessed are you among women,” it is almost an involuntary reflex of the heart and mind to envision the Virgin Mary. This declaration, echoing through centuries of art, scripture, and prayer, is inextricably woven into her identity. It is a title of singular honor, a divine acknowledgment that sets her apart in the grand narrative of salvation history. And in profound truth, this was not merely a poetic accolade but a reality that defined her existence—she truly was, and remains, uniquely blessed among all women.

This blessing, however, was not one of mere comfort or earthly ease. It was a blessing that arrived alongside a staggering responsibility, a calling that would demand unwavering faith, profound courage, and a heart willing to be pierced by sorrow. Her story begins not in a palace, but in the humble acceptance of a divine paradox. She was asked to believe the impossible: that she, a young woman of Nazareth, would conceive by the Holy Spirit and bear the very Son of God. Her simple, monumental response, “Let it be to me according to your word,” was the moment she embraced a destiny that would forever divide history into before and after.

The blessing unfolded through nine months of whispered rumors and the steadfast support of Joseph, through a journey to Bethlehem and the raw, sacred vulnerability of giving birth in a stable. It was the blessing of cradling infinite majesty in infant form, of nursing the one who created the universe, and of watching a carpenter's son grow in wisdom and stature. It was the joy of witnessing his first miracle at Cana, where her quiet confidence prompted the inauguration of his ministry.

Yet, this same blessing also led her to the foot of a cross, where the words "Blessed are you among women" must have echoed with a devastating and paradoxical weight. She stood there, as prophesied, with her soul pierced by a sword, watching her son, her Lord, sacrifice himself for the world she had helped to bring him into. Her blessing was complete, encompassing both the inexpressible joy of the Incarnation and the unimaginable agony of the Passion.

Thus, her story is the ultimate testament to what it means to be blessed by God. It is a narrative of grace that does not shield from pain but empowers through it; of a favor that invites one into the very heart of divine purpose, demanding everything and transforming the ordinary into the eternal. She is blessed not as a distant, untouchable figure, but as the foremost example of a human heart perfectly aligned with God's will—a testament to the glory that is born when a soul says "yes." This is her story.

*****

The historical record of Mary's childhood and adolescence remains, like that of most common people in first-century Judea, largely silent. The Gospels begin her story at its most pivotal moment. We are introduced to her as a young woman—historians and cultural anthropologists estimate she was likely between twelve and fourteen years old—living in the small, relatively obscure village of Nazareth in the region of Galilee. This youth was not unusual; in her time and culture, betrothal at this age was the custom, with the primary societal roles for women being wife and mother. This context makes the profound shame experienced by her relative, Elizabeth, who was well beyond childbearing years, deeply understandable.

The narrative opens with the divine interruption of the angel Gabriel, who appears to Mary with his astounding proclamation. It is a critical detail that Mary is at this time only betrothed to a man named Joseph. Betrothal (kiddushin) in ancient Jewish law was a legally binding covenant, more serious than a modern engagement, requiring a formal divorce to break. Yet, it was during this period of betrothal, before they had begun to live together as husband and wife, that this momentous event occurred.

Gabriel's message, that she would conceive and bear a son through the Holy Spirit, placed Mary in a position of incredible agency. Her "yes" was not a foregone conclusion. She possessed autonomy over her body and her future. Her response, "Behold, I am the servant of the Lord; let it be to me according to your word," is one of the most courageous declarations of faith recorded. In uttering it, she consciously accepted a path fraught with peril. An unwed pregnancy could have meant not only immense social ostracization but, according to the law of Moses (Deuteronomy 22:20-21), potential death by stoning for adultery. From her very first appearance in the biblical record, Mary is portrayed not as a passive vessel but as an active, brave participant in divine history, whose faith outweighed her fear.

Seeking solace, confirmation, and community, Mary undertook the long and arduous journey southward to the hill country of Judea. Her destination was the home of her relative Elizabeth, traditionally identified as an older cousin, in the village of Ein Karem, just west of Jerusalem. Historians believe this journey would have taken several days.

Upon Mary's arrival, a powerful and theological rich scene unfolds. As Mary calls out a greeting, Elizabeth, six months pregnant with the child who would be John the Baptist, is immediately filled with the Holy Spirit. The child within her womb "leaps for joy," a sign that transcends mere physical movement. This is a profound, prophetic recognition—the forerunner acknowledging the presence of the Messiah even from the womb. It foreshadows John's ministry decades later when he would see Jesus and declare, "Behold, the Lamb of God who takes away the sin of the world!" (John 1:29). This divine sign reveals the truth to Elizabeth, who responds with awe and humility, greeting Mary with the stunning title, "the mother of my Lord." Their meeting culminates in a beautiful outpouring of praise, including Mary's magnificent hymn of worship, now known as the Magnificat, a song that celebrates God's faithfulness to the humble and his revolutionary overturning of worldly power.

While it is certain that Joseph, being a "righteous man" who heeded his own divine dream, took Mary as his wife and that they did not consummate their marriage until after Jesus's birth, the exact timing of their wedding is unclear. Many scholars posit that the wedding occurred quietly after Mary returned from her three-month stay with Elizabeth. A subdued ceremony would have been prudent to avoid public scrutiny and questions about the timing of her pregnancy.

The biblical narrative is silent on the months of Mary's pregnancy, picking up again near its end. A decree from Emperor Augustus compelled Joseph to travel to Bethlehem, the City of David, to be registered in a Roman census. This journey, approximately 90 miles from Nazareth, would have been tremendously difficult for a woman in the advanced stages of pregnancy.

Contrary to the popular annual nativity plays, the Gospels do not describe a hostile innkeeper turning them away. Upon arriving in Bethlehem, Joseph would have naturally sought lodging in his ancestral family home. However, due to the census, the house was undoubtedly overcrowded with other returning relatives. With Mary going into labor, the main living quarters (katalyma), often translated as "inn," offered no privacy or appropriate space. They instead retreated to the home's lower level, a common feature in first-century Judean houses. This ground-floor area was typically used for storage and for housing the family's animals at night—not a dirty cave, but a clean, hollowed-out space that provided shelter and seclusion. With the flocks out to pasture during this season (historians place the birth likely in the autumn), this room would have been empty and available.

Here, Mary gave birth and laid her newborn son in a manger. This detail holds profound symbolic weight. A manger was not just any trough; it was often a stone structure also used as a table to inspect newborn lambs for the Temple sacrifices in nearby Jerusalem. Lambs had to be perfect, without spot or blemish, to be deemed worthy. In a breathtakingly surreal image, the infant Jesus, whom John would later call the ultimate sacrificial lamb, was laid upon this very table of examination—the spotless Lamb of God, born to take away the sin of the world, resting on the same manger that certified sacrificial worthiness.

The first visitors to witness this scene were local shepherds, summoned from their fields by a host of angels proclaiming the birth of the Messiah. The magi, or wise men, from the East, arrived much later, not at the stable, but at a "house" where the Holy Family was staying.

Forty days after the birth of her son, in meticulous obedience to the Mosaic Law, the Virgin Mary concluded her period of ritual purification. Following the commandments laid out in the book of Leviticus, the Holy Family undertook two sacred duties. First, on the infant's eighth day of life, he was circumcised, an act that formally incorporated him into the covenant of Abraham and, in accordance with custom, bestowed upon him the name announced by the angel: Jesus.

Then, for the second ritual, the family journeyed the five and a half miles north from their temporary home in Bethlehem to the holy city of Jerusalem. The Law required a mother to present a sacrifice at the Temple for her cleansing, offering a yearling lamb for a burnt offering and a young pigeon or turtledove for a sin offering. In a poignant detail that underscored the family's humble means, Mary and Joseph offered the provision allowed for those who could not afford a lamb: "a pair of turtledoves, or two young pigeons."

It was during this momentous visit to the Temple complex that divine providence intervened in a profound way. They were approached by a righteous and devout old man named Simeon, who lived in constant expectation of the "consolation of Israel." The Holy Spirit had revealed to him that he would not taste death until he had seen the Lord's Messiah with his own eyes. Moved by that same Spirit, he entered the Temple courts at precisely the right moment. His eyes fell upon the young couple and their infant. Overwhelmed with divine recognition, Simeon approached them, and with gentle, reverent hands, he took the child from Mary's arms. Cradling the promised salvation of all peoples, he lifted his voice to heaven in a prayer now known as the Nunc Dimittis: "Sovereign Lord, as you have promised, you may now dismiss your servant in peace. For my eyes have seen your salvation, which you have prepared in the sight of all nations: a light for revelation to the Gentiles, and the glory of your people Israel."

After blessing the young family, he turned specifically to Mary, his words taking a somber and prophetic tone. He foretold that the child was destined to cause the falling and rising of many in Israel and would be a sign spoken against. Then, speaking directly to the mother's heart, he delivered a heartbreaking prophecy: "And a sword will pierce your own soul too." This cryptic utterance foreshadowed the immense anguish she would one day endure, witnessing the rejection and crucifixion of her beloved son.

At that very hour, another faithful witness appeared: an elderly prophetess named Anna. A widow of great age, she had been married for seven years before her husband died, and had subsequently devoted the entirety of her long life—eighty-four years by some translations—to service in the Temple. She never left its courts, worshiping night and day with fasting and prayer. Drawn to the scene, she offered thanks to God and began to speak about the child to all in Jerusalem who, like her and Simeon, were looking forward to the redemption of the city.

The Gospel of Luke's narrative succinctly states that after fulfilling all the requirements of the Law, the family returned to their home in Nazareth. However, a fuller timeline suggests their return was significantly delayed. It is most likely they initially went back to Bethlehem, their ancestral town, where they remained for a period of nearly two years. The reasons for this extended stay are not explicitly stated but can be reasonably surmised. The arduous sixty-mile journey to Nazareth would have been incredibly difficult with a newborn. By the time Mary was strong enough to travel, the harsh winter rainy season and its muddy, impassable roads would have made the trip impractical. Joseph, a skilled carpenter, would have found ample work in the larger town of Bethlehem and its proximity to Jerusalem, making a prolonged stay both necessary and feasible.

It was during this prolonged residence in Bethlehem that a new chapter of the story unfolded. Mysterious wise men, Magi from the East, arrived in Jerusalem following a celestial sign. They inquired of King Herod the Great where they might find the one born "King of the Jews." The paranoid and ruthless king, deeply disturbed by this news, consulted his chief priests and scribes. They revealed the ancient prophecy from Micah pinpointing Bethlehem as the birthplace of the Christ. Herod deceitfully dispatched the

Magi to find the child and report back so he, too, could "worship him."

Guided by the star to the very house where the young child was, the Magi rejoiced. They presented their prophetic gifts: gold, honoring his kingship; frankincense, acknowledging his divinity; and myrrh, a spice used for burial, foreshadowing his sacrificial death. Divinely warned in a dream not to return to Herod, they departed for their own country by another route.

Enraged at being deceived by the Magi, Herod's fury crystallized into a monstrous decree. To eliminate this rival king, he ordered the slaughter of every male child in Bethlehem and its surrounding districts who was two years old and under, a horrific event that fulfilled the prophecy of Jeremiah and weeping echoed through Ramah.

But the Holy Family was already safe. Prior to the massacre, an angel of the Lord appeared to Joseph in a dream with an urgent command: "Get up! Take the child and his mother and escape to Egypt. Stay there until I tell you, for Herod is going to search for the child to kill him." Joseph immediately obeyed, undertaking a perilous journey to a foreign land to protect the Messiah. They remained there in safety for a decade, only returning to the land of Israel after the death of Herod the Great. Even then, fearing the rule of Herod's brutal son, Archelaus, in Judea, they were again divinely guided in a dream to withdraw to the relative safety of the remote Galilean village of Nazareth, thus fulfilling the prophecy that the Messiah would be called a Nazarene.

When the time for the Passover feast arrived, as was their devout custom, Joseph and Mary undertook the multi-day pilgrimage to the holy city of Jerusalem. This year was particularly significant, for their son, Jesus, was now twelve years of age—on the cusp of manhood according to Jewish tradition and soon to become a bar mitzvah, a "son of the commandment."

The journey to the city was filled with the excitement of a large caravan of relatives and friends from Galilee. The city itself was a breathtaking spectacle, teeming with thousands of pilgrims from across the diaspora, all there to fulfill their sacred duty. The Passover rituals in the Temple were observed with profound reverence, the scent of sacrifice hanging in the air alongside the unified prayers of a nation remembering its deliverance.

When the festivities concluded, the great caravan from Nazareth began its long trek north. In the bustling chaos of departure, with a large extended family group, it was easy to assume a child was with other relatives. Believing Jesus to be walking among their kin or close friends, Joseph and Mary traveled a full day's journey before settling for the evening. It was then, as families gathered around their cookfires, that his absence became alarmingly clear. A quick search among the traveling party yielded no sign of him. A cold dread, far colder than the night air, gripped their hearts.

Panic set in instantly. Every parent's nightmare was now their reality. Visions of the past flooded Mary's mind—the angelic announcements, the shepherds, the magi, and the terrifying flight from a vengeful King Herod. Now, Herod the Great was dead, but his son, Archelaus, ruled in Judea and was known for his equal brutality. The terrifying thought seized them: had the enemy they fled years before finally succeeded through his successor? Their search was frantic, immediate, and fruitless in the darkness.

With no other option, they turned back, retracing their steps toward Jerusalem, each mile stretching into an eternity of fear and guilt. The city they had left in celebration now represented a place of potential tragedy.

After three agonizing days of searching every conceivable place a young boy might be—the markets, the guest houses, the city gates—they finally thought to look in the Temple complex. There, in one of the chambers surrounding the outer court, they found him. He was not lost or hiding; he was seated calmly among the most esteemed teachers of the law—rabbis, scribes, and scholars known for their wisdom. The scene was not one of a child being lectured, but of a peer engaged in deep discourse. Jesus was both listening to them and asking them penetrating questions, and then offering insights that left these learned men astonished. His understanding of the Scriptures and his answers displayed a wisdom that far exceeded his years.

A wave of immense relief, followed by the raw emotion of the preceding days, washed over Mary. Rushing to him, her voice likely a mixture of tears and exasperation, she cried out, "Son, why have You done this to us? Look, Your father and I have sought You anxiously!"

Jesus' reply was not one of a defiant child, but a calm and sincere statement of identity and purpose that must have echoed strangely in the hallowed hall. He looked at them and asked, "Why did you seek Me? Did you not know that I must be about My Father's business?"

His words were a puzzle to them in that moment. Joseph, his earthly father who had protected and provided for him, stood beside Mary. Yet Jesus pointed to a higher lineage, a divine relationship. While they knew he was the promised Messiah from the events surrounding his birth, the full weight of his divinity—that he was consciously aware of his unique Sonship and his cosmic mission—had not yet been revealed to them in this way.

*****

The canonical Gospels are notably silent on a significant portion of Jesus's life, spanning approximately eighteen years from the return from Egypt to his public ministry. This period, often called the "hidden years," leaves many questions about the Holy Family's life in Nazareth. We know from passages like Matthew 13:55-56 that Mary and Joseph had other children: sons named James, Joseph (also called Joses), Simon, and Judas (or Jude), as well as unnamed daughters. A central question surrounds the timing of these births. Did they begin their family while still in Egypt, or did they wait until they returned to the land of Israel?

Most scholars and historians posit that they likely waited until after their return to Nazareth. This theory is rooted in Jewish law as described in Leviticus 12, which required a mother to offer a sacrifice for her purification after childbirth. Remaining in a foreign land like Egypt would have made fulfilling this important religious obligation difficult, if not impossible. It is therefore reasoned that Mary and Joseph, portrayed throughout scripture as devout Jews, would have awaited their return to their homeland to expand their family in accordance with Mosaic Law.

It is also during this long stretch of ordinary life in Nazareth that tradition and historical deduction suggest Joseph, the steadfast guardian of the Holy Family, passed away. His absence from the narrative of Jesus's adult life, particularly at the wedding at Cana and later at the crucifixion—events where a first-century Jewish father would typically be present—strongly implies he had died. This left Jesus, as the firstborn son, to assume the role of head of the household and caretaker for his mother, a responsibility that informs his actions later in the Gospel.

Mary re-emerges into the biblical narrative at a joyous occasion: the wedding in Cana (John 2:1-12). Accompanied by Jesus and his newly called disciples, she plays a pivotal role. Upon discovering the hosts have run out of wine—a major social disgrace—she immediately brings the problem to her son with simple trust: "They have no wine." Jesus's response, "Woman, what does this have to do with me? My hour has not yet come," has been debated for centuries.

To a modern reader, addressing one's mother as "Woman" sounds starkly disrespectful. However, historical and linguistic context reveals the opposite. In the first-century Greco-Roman world, the term "Gynai" (Woman) was a polite and respectful address, akin to "Madam" or "Ma'am," carrying dignity and formality without any inherent negativity. Jesus used the same term in a moment of profound tenderness from the cross. The latter part of his statement was not a refusal but a theological declaration that the timing of his public manifestation (his "hour") was under the divine authority of his Heavenly Father, not human prompting. Yet, embodying the commandment to honor one's parents, Jesus acquiesced to his mother's implicit faith. Mary, undeterred and demonstrating her own unwavering belief in him, instructed the servants, "Do whatever he tells you," setting the stage for his first miraculous sign.

Following the wedding, Mary, ever supportive, followed Jesus, his brothers, and his disciples to Capernaum, briefly sharing in the early days of his ministry.

The next time Scripture places Mary is at the darkest hour of her life: the foot of the cross. While the text only explicitly mentions her presence at the crucifixion itself (John 19:25-27), it is widely and logically believed that her anguish began much earlier. As a mother who had followed her son's ministry, it is inconceivable that she would have been absent during his trial, the abusive mocking, and the brutal flogging—a sight no parent should ever have to witness. Her strength throughout this ordeal is immense; she never fled but remained present, sharing in his suffering until his final breath.

Even in his agony, Jesus demonstrated his loving care for her. Seeing his mother and the disciple whom he loved (traditionally believed to be John, as James had already been martyred by the time the Gospel of John was written) standing nearby, he ensured her future security. In the patriarchal society of the time, a widowed woman with no husband or son to provide for her was left vulnerable. By entrusting Mary to the care of this beloved disciple and the disciple to her, saying, "Woman, behold, your son!... Behold, your mother!", Jesus performed a final act of filial devotion, establishing a new family bond rooted in discipleship.

The scriptures do not record a specific, intimate meeting between the resurrected Jesus and his mother, though it is a common and poignant subject of Christian contemplation. Surely, the one who appeared to many would have comforted the one who bore him. The last definitive glimpse we have of Mary is in the Upper Room after the Ascension, gathered with the eleven apostles, other women, and Jesus's brothers, devoting themselves to prayer in the days leading up to Pentecost (Acts 1:14). She, the first to believe, was now present at the birth of the Church. The Bible provides no record of her death, leaving her final days to Tradition and the respectful silence of history.

The legacy of Mary's faith extended through her other children. While Jesus's brothers were initially skeptical of his ministry (John 7:5), they became central figures in the early church after his resurrection. Two of them, James and Jude, are credited with authoring the New Testament epistles that bear their names. James, known as James the Just, became the highly respected leader of the church in Jerusalem, and his letter emphasizes practical faith and wisdom. Jude's short epistle is a vigorous defense of the faith against false teachings, forever linking the family of Nazareth to the foundational documents of Christianity.

A Girl Restored to Life and a Woman Healed

Before we journey forward to meet other named women in the Scriptures, it is vital to pause and honor the profound, quiet faith of two unnamed women whose lives were dramatically intertwined by a single, miraculous encounter. Their stories, nestled within one another in the Gospel accounts, present a powerful testament to faith in its most raw and desperate forms.

The first is known only by her relation to her father: the daughter of Jairus, a leader of the local synagogue. This position made Jairus a man of significant standing and religious authority within his community, a figure who would typically be expected to uphold tradition and maintain a cautious distance from a controversial rabbi like Jesus. Yet, when his beloved young daughter—his only child, as Luke's account tells us—fell gravely ill and lay at the brink of death, protocol and prestige crumbled before a father's love and despair. Pushing through the immense crowd that perpetually surrounded Jesus, Jairus did the unthinkable: he fell at the teacher's feet in an act of public worship. This was not a mere gesture of respect; it was a profound surrender of his own authority, an audacious declaration that he believed Jesus held power far beyond any earthly institution. Through desperate, choked pleas, he begged Jesus to come to his home, believing that a mere touch from the rabbi could snatch his daughter back from death itself. Moved by this

stunning display of faith from an unlikely source, Jesus agreed. The disciples and the pressing, curious crowd followed, a river of humanity flowing toward a house of mourning.
On the way, the procession was interrupted by a second woman, a figure existing in a state of complete social and religious opposite to Jairus's daughter. For twelve long years—the entire lifetime of the young girl they were rushing to save—this woman had suffered from a perpetual flow of blood. This condition rendered her ritually unclean according to Mosaic law, an outcast barred from worship and estranged from human touch. She was physically depleted, having spent her entire livelihood on physicians whose treatments had only worsened her suffering. Hearing the commotion of the crowd, a surge of hope cut through her exhaustion. We don't know how she knew it was Jesus, but a certainty settled in her spirit: if she could just touch the fringe of his garment—the tzitzit, the sacred tassels on a rabbi's cloak that symbolized God's commandments—she would be made well.

Summoning every last ounce of her strength, she pushed into the jostling throng. Ignoring the pain and the risk of publicly defiling others by her touch, she stretched out a trembling hand. The moment her fingers brushed the rough threads of his cloak, a surge of power—dunamis in Greek—flashed from Jesus and into her body. She knew instantly that her long nightmare was over; her hemorrhage had ceased.

Jesus, acutely aware of this divine energy leaving him, stopped and asked, "Who touched my clothes?" The question seemed absurd to the disciples, who pointed out that everyone in the dense crowd was pressing against him. But Jesus persisted, his gaze scanning the faces, seeking not an offender, but a recipient. Trembling with fear—not only from her miraculous healing but from the terror of having broken religious law and drawn public scrutiny—the woman fell before him. In front of everyone, she confessed her entire story. Instead of the rebuke she feared, she received a blessing that affirmed her worth and her faith. Jesus called her "Daughter," a term of intimate kinship, and declared, "Take heart; your faith has made you well. Go in peace." He lifted her from the dust, not only healing her body but restoring her dignity and her place in the community.

At that very moment, word arrived from the house of Jairus: "Your daughter is dead. Why trouble the Teacher any further?" The delay, prompted by an act of compassion, seemed to have cost a little girl her life. But Jesus turned to the heartbroken father and offered a new commandment: "Do not fear; only believe." Arriving at the home now filled with the cacophony of professional mourners' wails and the shrill sound of flutes, Jesus confidently dismissed the spectacle, stating, "Why are you making a commotion and weeping? The child is not dead but sleeping." Met with their scornful laughter, he cleared the room. Taking only the child's parents and his closest disciples, he entered where the girl lay. In a moment of breathtaking tenderness, he took her cold hand in his and spoke simple, life-giving words: "Little girl, I say to you, arise." Immediately, her spirit returned, and she got up and began to walk. Jesus, ever mindful of practical needs, instructed her stunned but overjoyed parents to give her something to eat.

In one extraordinary journey, Jesus demonstrated his power over chronic illness and ultimate death itself, responding not to social status, but to the unwavering, desperate faith of a grieving father and a desperate woman—faith that believed he was the source of all wholeness.

The Possessed Woman: Mary Magdalene

The figure of Mary Magdalene is one of the most recognizable, yet profoundly misunderstood, in the New Testament. For centuries, a persistent and inaccurate tradition has conflated her with the anonymous sinful woman who anoints Jesus' feet in Luke 7, leading to the widespread but erroneous label of her as a prostitute. This misconception was officially solidified by a series of sermons from Pope Gregory I in the 6th century. However, a careful reading of the biblical text itself reveals that the Gospels never identify Mary Magdalene as a prostitute or a woman of ill repute. This conflation is a historical error that overshadows her true, pivotal role as a premier disciple of Jesus.

Her origins, like those of many figures from antiquity, are shrouded in mystery. As her name suggests, she is believed to have come from Magdala, a prosperous fishing town on the western shore of the Sea of Galilee. The earliest definitive account of her life marks a moment of profound transformation: her healing by Jesus. The Gospel of Luke records that she was liberated from the torment of "seven demons." This phrase, while vague to modern readers, likely signified a severe and debilitating ailment, possibly a combination of physical, mental, and spiritual anguish. Some biblical scholars, analyzing the language and cultural context, have suggested this could point to severe substance abuse problems or profound psychological distress that was interpreted as demonic possession during that era. Significantly, she was not healed alone; she was part of a group of women, including Joanna (the wife of Herod's steward) and Susanna, who were also freed from similar afflictions.

This miraculous liberation forged an unbreakable bond of devotion. What is known with certainty is that these women, particularly Mary Magdalene, Joanna, and Susanna, became utterly devoted followers of Christ. In a culture where women were often financially dependent, these individuals were of independent means and became crucial financial patrons, supporting Jesus and his twelve disciples "out of their own means" as they traveled and ministered. This fact alone positions them not as peripheral figures, but as essential enablers of the ministry's daily operations.

While her story recedes into the background during much of Jesus' public ministry, Mary Magdalene re-emerges with heartbreaking courage at its climactic end. When virtually all the male disciples had fled in fear, Mary Magdalene was one of only three women who remained at the foot of the cross through the entirety of Jesus' agonizing crucifixion. She stood alongside Mary, the mother of Jesus, and Salome (the wife of Zebedee and mother of the apostles James and John). Their vigil did not end with Jesus' death. They followed Joseph of Arimathea to the garden tomb and witnessed the exact location where Jesus' body was laid to rest, a detail that would become critical hours later.

It was this same group of women, with Mary Magdalene explicitly named first in every Gospel account, who returned to the tomb at dawn on the first day of the week to anoint the body. Instead of a sealed grave, they found the stone rolled away and the tomb empty. They were met by two angels in dazzling garments who delivered history's most triumphant question: "Why do you seek the living among the dead? He is not here; he has risen!" The angels then reminded them of Jesus' own prophecies, and the women remembered his words. Filled with a mixture of fear and exhilarating joy, they ran to report this news to the Eleven Apostles.

Tragically, their testimony—the testimony of women, which held little legal or social weight in first-century Judaism—was dismissed by the apostles as "an idle tale." Only Peter and John ran to see for themselves. They found the empty tomb and the burial cloths, but left bewildered, convinced the body had been stolen. Mary Magdalene, however, could not leave. Overwhelmed by grief, she stayed behind alone, weeping. It was in this state of profound sorrow and devotion that she became the first person to encounter the resurrected Christ. Initially mistaking him for the gardener, she recognized him the moment he spoke her name: "Mary."

This moment is of immense theological significance. In a brilliant act of grace and a breaking of cultural norms, Jesus chose to reveal his resurrected self first not to Peter, his 'rock,' or to John, the 'beloved disciple,' but to a woman—a woman once possessed by seven demons. This act elevated the marginalized and established the witness of women as the foundational testimony of the Christian faith. Mary Magdalene, the healed disciple, thus became the first evangelist, the "Apostle to the Apostles," entrusted with carrying the good news of the resurrection to the very founders of the Church.

Her dedication did not end with this momentous event. She remained an active part of the early Christian community and was present in the Upper Room with the disciples and Jesus' mother when the Holy Spirit descended at Pentecost. While scripture provides no record of her later life or death, the unwavering narrative of her life paints a clear picture: from her day of healing onward, Mary Magdalene loved and served the Lord with her entire heart, soul, and resources. One can be certain that this faithful disciple, the first to witness the reality of resurrection, ultimately passed from this life into the eternal and loving arms of Christ Jesus.

The dead man's sisters: Mary and Martha

While their names are forever etched into the gospel narrative, the personal histories of Mary and Martha of Bethany remain largely shrouded in mystery. We are introduced to them not through a genealogy or a list of accomplishments, but through an intimate domestic scene: they are hosting Jesus, a revered but controversial rabbi, in their home in the village of Bethany, just two miles from Jerusalem. This initial encounter provides a profound and timeless lesson on devotion. Mary, captivated by Jesus's teaching, assumes the posture of a disciple, sitting at his feet to absorb his words. Martha, embodying the sacred duty of hospitality, is meanwhile "distracted with much serving," diligently working to honor her guests.

The scene culminates in a moment of classic sibling tension. Feeling the weight of her labors alone, Martha interrupts the gathering, directing her frustration not just at her sister, but at the Lord himself: "Lord, do You not care that my sister has left me to serve alone? Therefore tell her to help me." Jesus's response is gentle yet profoundly corrective, delivering a truth Martha likely did not expect to hear: "Martha, Martha, you are worried and troubled about many things. But one thing is needed, and Mary has chosen that good part, which will not be taken away from her." In this, Jesus elevates attentive devotion above anxious

activity, affirming that the primary call is to be with him, from which service then naturally flows.
The sisters reappear at the center of a crisis. Their brother, Lazarus, falls critically ill. Knowing Jesus's power and love for them, they send a simple, confident message: "Lord, behold, he whom You love is sick." Yet, in a move that perplexes human understanding, Jesus deliberately delays for two days after hearing the news. By the time he arrives in Bethany, Lazarus has been dead and entombed for four days—a significant detail, as Jewish tradition held that the soul departed from the body after three days, making his death, in the eyes of the community, irrevocable.

The sisters are surrounded by mourners who had traveled from Jerusalem, a testament to their standing in the community. Upon hearing Jesus is near, Martha, ever the woman of action, goes out to meet him on the road, while a grief-stricken Mary remains at home. Martha's greeting is a poignant mix of deep faith and profound sorrow: "Lord, if You had been here, my brother would not have died. But even now I know that whatever You ask of God, God will give You." Jesus offers her a supreme consolation: "Your brother will rise again." Martha, thinking in terms of orthodox Jewish eschatology, assumes he refers to the final resurrection. Her response, "I know that he will rise again in the resurrection at the last day," is theologically correct but misses the imminent miracle before her.

Jesus then makes one of the most monumental declarations of his identity: "I am the resurrection and the life. He who believes in Me, though he may die, he shall live. And whoever lives and believes in Me shall never die. Do you believe this?" In this moment, Martha articulates a breathtaking confession of faith, one of the clearest in the Gospels: "Yes, Lord, I believe that You are the Christ, the Son of God, who is to come into the world."

Martha then secretly summons Mary, who comes quickly, followed by the mourners assuming she is going to the tomb to weep. When Jesus sees her and the Jews weeping, he is deeply moved in spirit and troubled. The raw, shared grief of the moment is captured in the Bible's shortest and most human verse: "Jesus wept." Despite his divine foreknowledge of the coming miracle, he is fully present in the pain of his friends.

Arriving at the tomb—a cave with a stone laid against it—Jesus commands the stone be removed. Martha, the practical one, interjects with a grim reality check: "Lord, by this time there is a stench, for he has been dead four days." Jesus gently reminds her of his earlier promise: "Did I not say to you that if you would believe you would see the glory of God?" After a prayer thanking the Father, Jesus cries out with a loud voice, "Lazarus, come forth!" In an unprecedented and astonishing event, the dead man walks out, still bound in his grave clothes. Jesus's final command is one of liberation: "Loose him, and let him go."

The final scene featuring the sisters occurs six days before the Passover. Jesus and his disciples are once again guests in their home for a meal. Lazarus, a living testament to Jesus's power, reclines at the table with him, while Martha—true to her nature—serves. In an act of breathtaking devotion, Mary enters with an alabaster jar containing a pound of extremely costly spikenard oil. Breaking the jar, she anoints Jesus's feet and, in a gesture of deepest humility and love, wipes them with her hair, filling the house with the fragrance. When Judas Iscariot hypocritically complains about the waste, Jesus fiercely defends her, declaring that she has anointed him for burial and that this act of love would be remembered wherever the gospel is preached.

After this, Mary and Martha fade from the biblical narrative. Their deaths are not recorded, securing their legacy not in their end, but in their enduring witness: as beloved friends of Jesus, recipients of his comfort, witnesses to his power over death, and eternal examples of the dual calling to devotion and service, grounded in the belief that he is indeed the Christ, the Son of God.

Women of the new church

The descent of the Holy Spirit at Pentecost was nothing short of a spiritual earthquake, launching the Christian church into explosive, sustained growth. From its epicenter in Jerusalem, the gospel radiated outward with irresistible force, taking root in the hearts of people across Judea, Samaria, and unto the farthest reaches of the Roman Empire—throughout Greece, Asia Minor (modern Turkey), and even into the capital city of Rome itself. This rapid, massive expansion created an immediate and pressing need within the new communities of believers: a need for structure, for stewards to manage practical affairs, for teachers to deepen understanding of the faith, and for helpers to nurture the body of Christ.

It is crucial to understand that this work of building the church was not confined to the roles of apostles, evangelists, or those who handled money. The engine of the early church was powered by a vast array of gifts, many of which were the domain of faithful women who served with quiet, loving kindness. Their contributions, though sometimes overlooked in broad historical summaries, were indispensable. For instance, the Book of Acts tells the poignant story of a disciple in Joppa named Tabitha (also called Dorcas), renowned not for her preaching, but for her skillful hands and generous heart. When she died, the community was devastated. They urgently called for the Apostle Peter, and upon his arrival, they did not speak first of her theology but of her charity—showing him the very tunics and garments she had meticulously made for the poor widows. This was her ministry: a noble act of service that clothed the needy and strengthened the community. Peter, moved by their grief and her faithfulness, prayed and by God's power raised her from the dead, a miraculous affirmation of the value God places on such practical, compassionate service.

Similarly, we meet Priscilla, who alongside her husband Aquila, worked closely with the Apostle Paul as both tentmakers and ministry partners. She is specifically noted for helping to tutor the powerful but incomplete evangelist Apollos, explaining "the way of God more accurately." Furthermore, she and her husband risked their lives for Paul and hosted a church within their home. In his letter to the Romans, Paul gives direct and heartfelt credit to a host of women who were vital co-laborers in the gospel. He commends Phoebe, a deaconess and patron; Mary, who worked hard for the Romans; Junia, who was outstanding among the apostles; and the diligent trio of Tryphena, Tryphosa, and Persis, along with Julia and others. These were not passive spectators; they were active, essential participants in the ministry.

It is vital to remember that while the church was undoubtedly watered by the blood of martyred saints like Stephen, James, and later Peter and Paul, it was equally nurtured by the daily, loving kindness of countless women—both named and unnamed. Their stories are woven throughout the entire narrative of the Gospels and Acts, forming a foundational layer of support and faithfulness.

From the very beginning, there was Mary, the mother of Jesus, whose obedience made the Incarnation possible and who persevered as a disciple through his ministry and death. There were those healed and restored by Jesus, like Peter's mother-in-law, who immediately rose to serve; the woman with the issue of blood, whose faith made her whole; and Jairus's daughter, brought back to life. There were supporters like Mary Magdalene, Joanna, and Susanna, who provided for Jesus and the Twelve out of their own means. There were examples of faith like the persistent Syrophoenician woman and the generous widow who gave her last two mites.

Women were the last at the cross, beholding the crucifixion from a distance—Mary Magdalene, Mary the mother of James and Joses, Salome, and others. They were the first at the empty tomb, becoming the inaugural messengers of the resurrection. After the ascension, they were gathered in the upper room, praying constantly with the apostles.

As the church grew, so did their roles. Sapphira served as a tragic warning of hypocrisy, while many new women believers and Samaritan women were joyfully baptized into the faith. Lydia, a prosperous merchant, became the first convert in Europe and hosted the church in Philippi in her home. Rhoda, a servant girl, exhibited joyful faith upon Peter's miraculous release from prison. Philip's four daughters were known as prophetesses, and Priscilla continued her work as a teacher.

In short, the explosive growth of the early church was not a phenomenon sustained solely by the travels of its most famous male apostles. It was equally fueled by the indispensable, multifaceted, and often courageous contributions of women. They served as disciples, healers, witnesses, financiers, hostesses, teachers, deacons, artisans, and prophets. Their faithful service in both dramatic and mundane ways provided the practical and spiritual sustenance that allowed the church to not only grow but to thrive, firmly establishing a legacy of integral partnership in the work of the gospel.

*****

It is imperative to note that the active and foundational role women held within the early church did not simply conclude with the closing of the biblical canon. While it is historically accurate that women's formal leadership roles were systematically suppressed in the subsequent centuries (particularly from 100 AD onward), this was a consequence of evolving human institutions, not a divine mandate. This suppression was significantly, though not solely, advanced by the actions of ecclesial bodies like the Council of Nicaea in 325 AD. It is crucial to clarify that the Council did not issue a single, explicit decree aimed exclusively at suppressing women; rather, its canons—coupled with the broader theological, structural, and social consolidation it catalyzed—solidified a clerical hierarchy that increasingly excluded women from positions of authority, thereby contributing profoundly to the marginalization of their voices within the emerging institutional church.

However, this book is not primarily concerned with the history of that "institutional church." Its focus is on the true, universal Church—whose foundations were laid at the crucifixion and resurrection of Christ, whose early roots were watered by the blood of martyred saints like Stephen, Paul, and Peter, and whose initial growth was tirelessly nurtured by the loving, hardworking hands of countless women. Figures like the deacon Phoebe, the teacher Priscilla, and the benevolent maker of garments, Tabitha, were not peripheral but essential to the Church's vitality. This legacy of indispensable female contribution did not vanish; it persisted, often in the margins of official record-keeping, and one powerful exemplar of this enduring spirit is Margaret Fell Fox.

In the 17th century, Margaret Fell, much like Priscilla in the first century, dedicated her home, Swarthmoor Hall in England, to God's service, regularly hosting traveling ministers and providing a safe haven for religious discourse. In 1652, she met the radical preacher George Fox, the founder of the Religious Society of Friends, known as Quakers. His message of the "Inner Light"—the belief that Christ speaks directly to every individual without the need for an ordained priesthood—resonated deeply with her. Margaret swiftly became a central pillar of the movement, hosting meetings, advocating fiercely for religious freedom, and leveraging her considerable intellect and social standing to defend the Friends.

Her most profound contribution was her written work. In 1666, while imprisoned for her beliefs, she penned a seminal tract titled Women's Speaking, Justified by the Scriptures. In this powerful, systematic argument, Fell meticulously explored the entirety of the Bible, from Eve to the Marys at the tomb, to champion the right of women to preach, teach, and hold authority within the ministry. She asserted that true spiritual authority flowed from the Spirit of God, which falls upon all believers irrespective of gender, thus advocating for a radical equality of the sexes in the spiritual realm. The patriarchal world of Restoration England was unprepared for such a formidable woman. After the death of her first husband, Thomas Fell, in 1658, Margaret's activism led to her arrest in 1664. She was sentenced to life imprisonment for refusing to swear an oath and for hosting Quaker meetings. Yet, in a testament to the scriptural promise of liberation she held dear, she was released by order of King Charles II in 1668. She subsequently married George Fox and continued to travel and minister alongside him until his death in 1691, leaving an indelible mark on Christian thought regarding women's roles.

Another woman whose service to the Church continues to resonate in worship services around the globe is the remarkable hymnwriter Fanny Crosby. Born Frances Jane Crosby in 1820, she became blind in infancy due to a doctor's error. Rather than succumbing to limitation, she cultivated prodigious talents in poetry and music. Over her lifetime, under various pseudonyms, she authored a staggering corpus of work: over 9,000 hymns, more than 1,000 secular poems, four published books of poetry, and two best-selling autobiographies. Her ability to translate deep theological truths into accessible, emotionally powerful language made her hymns immensely popular. Masterpieces like "Blessed Assurance," "Jesus, Keep Me Near the Cross," "Safe in the Arms of Jesus," and "To God Be the Glory" are not mere historical artifacts; they are living, breathing elements of modern worship, sung by millions to this day. Through her words, Fanny Crosby's voice, silenced by blindness but amplified by faith, continues to lead the church in praise, proving that service to God takes countless forms, each one vital to the body of Christ.

*****

While we rightly celebrate the foundational contributions of women like Margaret Fell Fox, whose theological writings defended the concept of the "Inner Light" in all believers, and Fanny Crosby, whose prolific hymnody gave the church a voice for worship, their roles, though vital, often operated within acknowledged societal boundaries. This naturally leads to a more pointed inquiry: Beyond writing and foundational support, did women ever truly step into the pulpit itself? Were there women who stood as recognized preachers, publicly expounding the Word of God with authority?

The answer is a resounding yes, and one of the most formidable examples is Catherine Booth. Born Catherine Mumford in Ashbourne, England, in 1829, she was forged in the crucible of a rigidly patriarchal religious culture that systematically barred women from leadership and public teaching roles. Although she is most famously remembered as the co-founder of the Salvation Army alongside her dynamic husband, the revivalist William Booth, this title scarcely captures the profound theological and social revolution she personally championed.

Her journey into ministry was sparked not in a seminary, but in solitude and physical suffering. As a teenager, a severe spinal curvature confined her to bed for extended periods. Rather than succumbing to idleness, she transformed her sickroom into a sanctuary of intense study. It is reported that she read the entire Bible cover-to-cover eight times before her twelfth birthday. This deep immersion in Scripture was supplemented by the works of theological giants like Charles Finney and John Wesley. Their writings on personal holiness, social justice, and fervent evangelism ignited a fire within her, compelling her toward a public calling long before society deemed it acceptable.

Her social conscience was equally acute. She developed a fierce concern for the ravages of alcoholism, a blight particularly destructive to working-class families, and became a lifelong advocate for total abstinence. It was, in fact, this shared passion for temperance that first connected her to William Booth. Upon hearing him recite a powerful poem titled "The Grog-seller's Dream," she was captivated by both his message and his conviction. They married in 1855, forming what would become one of history's most potent ministerial partnerships. Catherine was herself an ordained Methodist minister and served for three years as a traveling evangelist, yet she continually chafed against the constraints placed upon her gender.

Her central struggle was with the deeply entrenched doctrine that women were biblically forbidden to preach. She viewed this not merely as a social injustice but as a theological error that crippled the church by silencing half of its gifted members. This belief, she argued, was a "blunder" and an "embarrassment" to God's work. With William's full encouragement—a critical factor in her empowerment—Catherine mounted a formidable intellectual defense. In 1859, she penned Female Ministry: Woman's Right to Preach the Gospel, a short but blisteringly logical and scripturally saturated treatise. She meticulously deconstructed traditional arguments against women preachers, asserting that the Holy Spirit's gifting was the sole requirement for ministry, irrespective of gender.

The theory soon became practice. In 1860, during one of William's services, she could remain silent no longer. Overcoming immense personal trepidation, she asked to speak. From that pulpit, she delivered an extemporaneous sermon that was so powerfully anointed and well-received that her reputation as a preacher instantly spread, with some contemporaries noting that her oratory gifts soon rivaled and even surpassed those of her famous husband.

Thereafter, she became William's full partner in the pulpit, preaching revival throughout England. Their joint efforts built the Christian Mission from a small East London endeavor into a powerful movement. This organization, dedicated to both evangelical preaching and radical social action among the poor and outcast, was reorganized in 1878 and given its iconic name: The Salvation Army.

Within this Army, Catherine was affectionately and respectfully known as the "Army Mother." This title reflected her unwavering leadership, her maternal care for converts, and her fearless faithfulness to a ministry that seamlessly blended preaching the Gospel with addressing societal ills. Her groundbreaking legacy is not confined to history books; it is vibrantly alive today in the work of the Salvation Army, which operates in more than 133 countries, continuing her fight for souls and social justice, led by men and women on equal footing—a direct fulfillment of Catherine Booth's vision.

*****

Catherine Booth's seminal work, "Female Ministry: Woman's Right to Preach the Gospel," stands as a powerful and meticulously argued theological treatise that refutes the prohibition of female preachers, not as a legitimate biblical mandate, but as a profound and long-standing theological error born of misinterpretation and cultural bias.

To fully appreciate her argument, one must first understand its foundation. Booth strategically opens her polemic not with a defensive posture, but with an assertive claim on biblical prophecy. She cites the words of the prophet Joel, as echoed by the Apostle Peter on the Day of Pentecost in Acts 2:17: "Your sons and your daughters shall prophesy." This is a deliberate and powerful opener, establishing from the outset that the divine intention, as revealed at the very birth of the Christian church, includes the Spirit-empowered proclamation of God's word by women. It is an irrefutable affirmation of spiritual equality.

Booth then masterfully addresses the primary societal objection: that a woman preaching is "unnatural." She dismantles this claim not merely with abstract theory but with concrete, historical evidence. She provides a compelling roster of pious and effective female preachers and evangelists who preceded her, including figures like:

Madame Guyon, a renowned French writer. Lady Maxwell, a prominent figure in the Methodist revival in Scotland. Susanna Wesley, the "Mother of Methodism," who led prayer meetings for hundreds and profoundly influenced her sons, John and Charles. Mary Fletcher, a powerful Methodist preacher. Elizabeth Fry, the famous Quaker prison reformer and minister. Alongside Mrs. Smith, Mrs. Whiteman, and Miss Marsh.

By pointing to their fruitful ministries, Booth argues that if such impactful, Gospel-centered work is the result, it cannot be deemed "unnatural" but must be recognized as God-ordained.

The crux of her theological argument, however, is her masterful exegesis of the two most commonly cited "clobber" passages: 1 Corinthians 14:34-35 and 1 Timothy 2:11-12. Her treatment of the former is particularly brilliant. She presents the verses in full, where Paul instructs women to "keep silent in the churches" and to be "under obedience." Rather than dismissing them, she engages in a rigorous contextual analysis.

She first highlights a seeming contradiction by pointing the reader to 1 Corinthians 11:1-15, where Paul provides instructions for how women should pray and prophesy in church—an act that inherently involves speaking. Booth poses a piercing, almost facetious rhetorical question: "Will any one maintain that Paul here refers to the same kind of speaking as before? If so, we insist on his supplying us with some rule of interpretation which will harmonize this unparalleled contradiction and absurdity."

Her conclusion is that the speaking forbidden in Chapter 14 is categorically different from the prophesying permitted in Chapter 11. She argues that Paul is not silencing all speech but specifically targeting disruptive, argumentative, and arrogant speech that was causing chaos in the Corinthian worship service. This kind of speaking—"questioning, finding fault, disputing... attempts to usurp authority over men by setting up their judgment in opposition to them"—was an act of disobedience that no Spirit-filled woman would engage in. To bolster this linguistic argument, she quotes the Reverend J.H. Robinson, who provides deep scholarly insight into the original Greek words and their context.

Booth sums up her position succinctly: the command was not for absolute silence but for a refraining from speech that was inconsistent with a spirit of obedience and peace, specifically that which would "ruffle their tempers, and occasion an unamiable volubility of speech." She further strengthens her case by reminding readers of the numerous women—like Philip's four prophetic daughters (Acts 21:9) and Priscilla, who instructed Apollos (Acts 18:26)—who served openly in the early church.

She then turns to 1 Timothy 2:11-12, arguing that Paul's injunction against a woman teaching or usurping authority over a man has a similar context-specific meaning. While Booth's own analysis focuses on the principle of disruptive behavior, we must look at a critical historical layer that adds immense weight to her argument: the cultural context of Ephesus.

Timothy was leading a church in a city dominated by the worship of Artemis (Diana), whose spectacular temple was one of the Seven Wonders of the World. This was a female-centric cult where women held ultimate religious authority as high priestesses. The new Christian community in Ephesus was thus likely contending with influential pagan women who were attempting to import their familiar, dominant religious roles and possibly heretical ideas into the church. When read through this lens, Paul's command takes on a specific, localized meaning. He is not issuing a universal ban on all female teaching; he is instructing Timothy to quell disruptive arguments and prevent the dissemination of false doctrine by these specific Gentile converts from the Artemis cult, telling them to learn quietly rather than dominate the conversation with unsound teachings.

When synthesizing Catherine Booth's exhaustive scriptural analysis with this historical understanding, her core thesis becomes undeniable: the traditional interpretation that universally forbids women from preaching is an error. The biblical texts, properly understood in their historical and literary context, do not support such a blanket prohibition. Paul's instructions were situational, aimed at preserving order and orthodoxy in specific first-century churches, not at silencing the Spirit-empowered ministry of women for all time.

In conclusion, Catherine Booth's work systematically demonstrates that the biblical case for silencing women is built on a misinterpretation of culturally specific passages. The consistent witness of Scripture, from Joel and Acts to the ministry of women like Phoebe, Priscilla, and the four daughters of Philip who prophesied, is one of inclusion and calling. Therefore, Sisters, if the Holy Spirit calls you into service listen and act. From the most visible pulpit to the most humble task, every role is sacred when done in obedience to God's Spirit. The call to preach is not based on gender, but on gifting and divine appointment, a truth Catherine Booth championed not as a modern innovation, but as a recovery of authentic biblical practice.

www.ingramcontent.com/pod-product-compliance
Lightning Source LLC
LaVergne TN
LVHW010651110826
845149LV00014B/3040

* 9 7 9 8 9 9 6 0 4 4 3 1 3 *